the road to
PARENTHOOD

TRANSFORMING THE STRUGGLES OF INFERTILITY
INTO THE BLESSINGS OF ADOPTION

Barbara Robertson

The Road to Parenthood
Transforming the Struggles of Infertility Into the Blessings of Adoption
Barbara Robertson
Three Peace Press

Published by Three Peace Press, Ashland, Oregon

Editor: Cindy Mosher

Cover and Interior design: DavisCreativePublishing.com

Publisher's Cataloging-in-Publication

Names: Robertson, Barbara (Robertson Horner), author.

Title: The road to parenthood : transforming the struggles of infertility into the blessings of adoption / Barbara Robertson.

Description: Ashland, Oregon : Three Peace Press, [2025]

Identifiers: LCCN: 2025923891 | ISBN: 9798993913506 (paperback) | 9798993913513 (ebook)

Subjects: LCSH: Parenthood. | Adoption. | Adoptive parents. | Infertility. | Parenting. | Families. | BISAC: FAMILY & RELATIONSHIPS / Life Stages / General. | FAMILY & RELATIONSHIPS / Alternative Family. | FAMILY & RELATIONSHIPS / Multicultural & Multiracial Families.

Classification: LCC: HQ755.8 .R63 2025 | DDC: 306.874--dc23
2025

Much like a butterfly's metamorphosis, our journey to build a family was one of patience, pain, and hope—until at last we emerged, transformed and more beautiful than we ever imagined possible.

Table of Contents

Preface

This is the story of a journey—not just across continents, but through the depths of heartbreak, hope, and, ultimately, transformation. I am the woman at the heart of these pages, having faced storms that would break most, enduring five miscarriages, two dangerous ectopic pregnancies, and the soaring hope—and repeated disappointment—of seven in vitro fertilization attempts. For years, I carried not just the silent ache of loss, but also the relentless pressure to keep going, to try again, to fight through tears, fear, and uncertainty.

Each loss left its mark. Each failed attempt felt like the closing of another door. But this is not a story about surrender. It is a testament to resilience and perseverance, to the courage to let go of one path and seek another, even when the heart is raw and fragile.

When biology failed me, love did not. Opening myself to the wider world, I embarked on the path of adoption, navigating the complex, beautiful, and sometimes heartbreaking realities of building a family across borders and cultures. From the bustling streets of Saigon to the sunlit hills of Addis Ababa, I found our children—one in Vietnam and two in Ethiopia—and with them, an extraordinary new definition of mother, family, and home.

This book is for anyone who has dreamed, grieved, and hoped again. It's about forging family not just through blood, but through mama bear love, unwavering faith, and the belief that family is not only what we're given, but what we create.

Section 1

The Dream of Motherhood

As women, we are given the gift to create life. The ability to grow a tiny human inside our womb and raise it up to be an amazing adult. As a little girl, this was a dream that I wanted so very much. I just knew that this was my blueprint to unravel in this glorious world that God created.

Chapter 1

Did you ever have wild dreams as a kid? When I was little, I dreamed of being a mom to fourteen kids! Crazy right? I was what my mother called "The Pied Piper of the Neighborhood"—as a young girl, I was the one who organized neighborhood games, dreamed up imaginative play, and turned living rooms into magical places with puppet shows, plays, and singing. I was always eager to share laughter, invent new worlds, and inspire others to see the joy in the world.

I wanted to be a mom because I was creative, full of personality, and playful. I loved gathering the kids in the cul-de-sac to do fun activities such as tubing down the drainage ditch in inner tubes, creating carnivals, parades, Christmas caroling, and dressing up as the Easter bunny. Motherhood, to me, felt like the great adventure where all those qualities could truly shine.

Being creative, I imagined motherhood would be filled with opportunities to craft, bake, build forts, and invent fantastical stories. I saw myself as the architect of happy childhood memories, creating days full of color and magic. The thought of watching a child's eyes light up as their imagination took flight was thrilling. I looked forward to making Halloween costumes, science experiments in the kitchen, and rainy days transformed by the magic of imagination.

A bubbly personality, too, played its part in fueling my dream. I've always been able to connect with people, lift spirits, and to guide with both strength and gentleness. I believed those traits would help me encourage my children to be confident, compassionate, and kind. I truly hoped to be not just a parent, but a role model and a trusted friend—someone they could laugh with, come to with concerns, and rely on for support.

Most of all, I wanted to share the pure fun that comes from being playful. Life is hard enough, but I knew that as a mom I could help make it softer, lighter—at least for the time being. Whether it was silly dances in the kitchen, pillow fights before bedtime, or impromptu picnics in the yard, I wanted my children to grow up feeling that wonder and joy could be found anywhere.

Once I became a teenager I began babysitting. This gave me the knowledge that two kids were easier to take care of than five. With this understanding, I began to realize that fourteen kids would probably be a bit much, and I lowered my expectation to no more than seven kiddos. Taking care of kids helped me realize early on that motherhood requires more than just fun and play. It requires patience, resilience, sacrifice, and a strong, devoted type of love. Still, I felt that creativity, charisma, and playfulness are gifts that turn the challenges of parenthood into a journey of endless possibility and hope. I knew I wouldn't be a perfect mom, but I was sure that by being myself—creative, bubbly, and playful—I could give my children a joyful place to grow and thrive. And that would be the greatest adventure of all.

Ever since my teenage years, through college and beyond, the dream of becoming a mother was always close to my heart. Even while I was dating, I knew I wanted to start a family of my own. Eventually, I met a partner—the man I knew I wanted to share my life with and start a family. He was tall and handsome, with strikingly beautiful, long red curls. More than that, he was sentimental and romantic, with a quick sense of humor, a loving heart, and a warm, playful manner around children.

One evening while we were out to dinner, the conversation turned serious as we talked about marriage, our hopes for the future, and children. I didn't hold back about my hopes for motherhood. We laughed and dreamed together, and by the time we were married—having written our own vows—it felt only natural to make plans for our future family. On our honeymoon, we even spent one evening making a list of all the names we'd consider for our future kids.

As life moved forward, I graduated from grad school with my Master of Science in Elementary Education, and we both felt ready to take the next step. We had already talked about our hopes for a family, agreeing that we wanted at least two children—we would see what the future held for us after that. With our hearts full of anticipation and excitement (and our list of baby names from our honeymoon tucked away), we decided it was finally time to start the adventure of parenthood together.

Our plans to start a family were underway, but a move to Vermont took center stage. My husband had just completed his Bachelor of Science in Psychology and wanted to go to grad school at the University of Vermont. We packed every-thing and drove across the United States, stopping along the way to see the sites such as the Grand Canyon. We arrived in time to settle in for a gorgeous New England fall. I found work as a substitute teacher and at a local bookstore. My husband found a job in a local restaurant as a waiter. We were enjoying our new life in the small town of Winooski, just across the river from the bustling town of Burlington.

About four months into living there, I had a missed period. I noticed that my breasts were getting bigger, and I thought for sure that I was pregnant. My husband thought it was my imagination. I decided it could just be wishful thinking, and so I waited a while longer before pursuing a pregnancy test. One winter day, while I was working as a substitute teacher in a nearby elementary school, I started to have excruci-ating, sharp pains in my pelvis. At first, I thought it was just gas, but the pain seemed lower in my uterus, and I began to worry that it might have something to do with the possibility of being pregnant. The pain was so sharp that I was unable to continue my work and had to go home early.

The pain would not subside, and I insisted on going to the hospital. My husband finally succumbed to my pleas and drove me to the emergency room. By the time I had been admitted, the first question was, "Are you pregnant?" I told the nurse that I didn't know for sure, but thought I was. I was then given a cup to pee in, and we waited patiently in the lobby for the results. Within an hour the nurse came out and told us the test came back positive.

I was both elated and scared. My childhood dream was finally happening, but I couldn't stop worrying about the pain and what that might mean. After the pregnancy test, they had to admit me for more testing. I was told I was 10 weeks pregnant. I was trying my best to keep an optimistic view, but the sharp, stabbing pain was not ceasing. The doctor came back with the newest test results that identified the fetus was not in my uterus, but in my fallopian tube. I had an ectopic pregnancy. Having never heard of such a thing, I was unclear what this meant for me. The fetus was growing in my fallopian tube. It had not made it into my uterus. I remember feeling so scared—almost paralyzed by the uncertainty of what might happen next. Would I lose the pregnancy? My husband seemed more focused on the practical aspects of my pregnancy, expressing concerns about becoming parents. Maybe that's normal, but I felt hurt and confused given we had begun plans to start a family.

The doctor said that this could be life-threatening and I would need surgery to remove the fetus from the tube. My first thought was whether it was possible to save the fetus and move it into my uterus. The doctor told me that they would try their best to save the developing baby and the tube, but there was no guarantee. I would most likely die if the surgery were not performed. My life was the first concern at this point.

I was being prepped for surgery when the nurse left, and I told my husband I was hungry. He went down to the cafeteria and grabbed me a bagel. A few minutes after I started to eat it, the anesthesiologist came in and said he could not administer the anesthesia for another six hours since I had eaten. We had not even thought that was a thing. This meant six more hours of pain. Not a happy moment for me.

My husband had to start his shift at the restaurant, leaving me alone with no family nearby. I had never been so frightened in my life. At the time, I felt abandoned, as though he had less concern for my health and more for the logistics. It was a hurt that would take time to process and unravel.

When I awoke from the anesthesia, I felt panicked because I remembered what had just happened. Immediately I called for a nurse. I asked in a terrified tone how my baby was. He told me he would get the doctor. When the doctor came in, her kind eyes looked down at me, and she spoke with a gentle voice, expressing regret that she was unable to save the fetus. She further explained that my fallopian tube had ruptured, and they had to remove it. This meant that I only had one fallopian tube now. Tears welled up in my eyes. My heart ached from this unbelievable loss, and I was veiled in a deep grief I had never known before. How could life be so cruel?

What would that mean for me getting pregnant again?

I would need to have some more tests done soon to determine if the other tube had any blockage. The next test would be a hysterosalpingogram (HSG), a procedure I couldn't even pronounce. I took a few weeks to recover from the surgery and work through my loss before I went back for the HSG—an X-ray procedure that uses a blue dye, injected into the vagina to identify blockages or irregularities.

Before the procedure began I was told that usually there is little pain; however, on rare occasions, some patients had reported a high degree of pain. When the procedure started, I soon realized I was the rare occasion. The pain ripped through my body, making it hard to breathe. I screamed and gasped for air, feeling like I was going to heave. I had never experienced such a high intensity of pain. I figured that if the test results were favorable, I would find comfort in this excruciating procedure.

When the results came back, I was relieved to find out that my only fallopian tube had no blockage and that I could still get pregnant every other ovulation. However, the results showed that I had an irregularly shaped uterus. The doctor said that my uterus is T-shaped. She assured me that this was not going to be an issue.

At the time I did not fully understand what this meant. But I stayed focused on the message that I could still get pregnant.

Chapter 2

The emotional and physical strain from the ectopic pregnancy, along with the fear of the unknown, continued to weigh on me. But the normalcy of going back to work helped ease the weight and keep my mind busy. Substitute teaching was a great way to escape my grief since I could pour my energy and care into the young minds of the children I taught.

My teaching job only paid minimum wage in Vermont, so I had a second job working at a bookstore. When I went back to work at the bookstore, my coworkers were very sympathetic about my loss. I soon found out that one of my coworkers was pregnant and was hesitant to talk about it around me. However, I eventually found out. I know she was just being sensitive to my recent loss, yet I felt a bit embarrassed that she had kept it from me. I was quite excited for her, but I didn't want to be treated like a wounded puppy. In my mind, I was a survivor—not a victim. Grief was hard, yet necessary. Baby A was not going to keep me from becoming a mom.

Two weeks later, my mom called to tell me that my grandma had died. She had been my last living grandparent. Loss is never easy, but the grief I was already feeling from the failed pregnancy had now increased tenfold. I was feeling so sad for my mom losing her mother. I was confused why loss had to follow loss. This seemed so unfair. Why was life flourishing for others while I was drowning in sorrow? Sometimes life doesn't make sense. This was too much for me to compre-hend so close together. I called my childhood best friend and lamented to her. She invited me to come down to visit her in Florida for some rest and relaxation to reset my emotional thermometer.

After the sadness of going through the ectopic pregnancy and now losing my grandmother, my time in Florida offered a gentle reset—helping me gradually shift my focus toward new opportunities and beginning my job search. I soon began applying for teaching positions for the following school year. I applied for almost forty openings throughout Vermont. I was so confident I would find a job. Eventually, I got a call for an interview. I was so excited to go. I thought this would be my opportunity to start again. When I entered the room, there was a large table full of interviewers. I felt my body freeze—my mind went blank. I couldn't even form coherent words. This had never happened to me before. I had always done well in interviews. Our body can hold trauma longer than we even realize at times. I guess this was my body's way of showing me I had not worked through all the grief. I was not ready to let go and move on.

Unfortunately, no other schools called me for an interview. I just could not continue to substitute teach for minimum wage. I wanted to start my career. I wanted to be busy creating my own classroom. I was in need of time to get over my loss before moving forward with starting a family. Vermont was a lovely place, but it held sad memories and little future at this time. I began searching for a job outside of Vermont. While we had moved here for my husband to pursue his graduate degree, life circumstances kept him from completing his goal, leaving us with little reason to stay in Vermont. We decided to embark on Plan B.

The West Coast was calling me back and I went to live with my mom for the summer while looking for a job. My husband continued to work in Vermont while I searched for work. The plan was for him to move our things once we had a new destination. I applied for jobs in Portland while substitute teaching for twice as much as minimum wage. I also applied for jobs at a school district in California. I had two interviews, one for an Oregon school and one in California. The interview in California was over the phone initially and then a second interview took place in Sacramento. I flew down to Sacramento and fell in love with the idea of teaching kids of other cultures. I was offered a job and got to choose which school and grade I wanted. I chose a school with a large population of Hispanic and many Russian kids, teaching third grade.

By October, my husband moved our stuff from Vermont to a house in Sacramento. It was a sweet Victorian in midtown. For a while, I was content with just getting my kid-fix at work and coming home to an empty nest. Being a DINK (double income, no kids) had a lot of benefits. Between my life as an educator with time to socialize and travel, I was comfortable not having kids for another two years.

Then the "I am in my thirties" clock started ticking. Although my husband may have wanted to delay starting a family, I felt like I didn't want to push my luck. So, we started trying. By then we had bought a home and renovated it. I was now 35 years old. We were settled and ready to start trying—perhaps

I was more eager than my husband, though he supported our family plans.

I got pregnant again in the early 2000s. This time I took a home test as soon as my period was late. I wanted to be at the top of my game this time. I was too worried to wait. The excitement had me at the store purchasing a test as soon as I suspected the possibility of a pregnancy. The test was positive and we were so thrilled! I immediately made an appointment with my OBGYN. I couldn't wait to see that cute little peanut. My doctor set me up on the examination table and began the ultrasound—there was a heartbeat.

This was so amazing to see, but then the memory of my ectopic pregnancy came flooding back and I felt fearful. Although I was ecstatic, there was a bit of worry about another loss. The mixed feelings were creating some ambivalence that I tried hard to shake off. I needed to stay optimistic for the baby. I felt like I might jinx it if I told anyone, so I kept it quiet and decided to tell close family, but not to tell my friends. About eight weeks in, I went back to see my doctor and there was no heartbeat—I miscarried. I knew that I could try again, but the ache was still very real. The tears once again fell from my eyes. Another quiet mourning was upon me.

The following year, we were skiing at Mt. Hood in Oregon during Christmas break. We were staying at a lodge for two days of skiing before going to spend the holiday with our families. The powder was amazing, and I was getting my adrenaline fix when I launched off a jump, caught some major air, and took a face plant. Ouch! But that is part of the fun. It was an epic ski trip with powder and sunshine, not a care in the world.

A couple days later I was in a bit of discomfort and realized I was late for my period, so I took a home test. I was pregnant again. A bit surprised yet happy, I went to see a local doctor. It turned out that I was pregnant, but in the midst of another miscarriage. The disappointment of a third miscarriage enveloped a shadow over the Christmas holiday for me. I never thought that becoming a mom would be so tragic. Although I had experienced this type of loss before, it didn't make it any less painful. I tried to explain it away. I convinced myself it was because of my skiing accident. But my can-do attitude took over and I told myself—I wasn't going to let this keep me from trying again.

So here I was at 37 years old and my childhood dream of having fourteen children was not likely to come true. But I wanted to have at least one child. I had thought about adoption when I was younger, but by now my ego wanted to have a baby that looked like me. The idea of creating life was such a powerful pull in my body that I wasn't ready to give up. Each miscarriage brought grief; however, I saw myself as a survivor, not a victim, and pulled myself up by the bootstraps once more.

Being 37 put me in the category of advanced maternal age. I wasn't sure why the world put this on us women. I kept hearing about celebrities who had waited until their late 30s and were having children. My sister had her sixth child at the age of 44. In the Bible, Sarah had a baby at about 90 years old. What did these doctors know? Why could men create a child late in life? This advanced maternal age was grossly unjust as far as I was concerned. I was not going to let doctors determine my fate. My personal doctor did not seem too concerned at this point, since all the tests showed everything looked ok to continue trying naturally, without intervening medically. I was healthy and our stats looked good. I unabashedly told myself that I could have a baby despite being older, so I put this off for another year.

Why would I wait another year? Maybe there was some subconscious reluctance. Perhaps it was denial, though deep down I was scared I would be a childless woman, and my worth would be less than my friends and family who were mothers. I spent my time immersed in my job and being on committees, creating more school plays, and developing our school into an arts and sciences charter. But the clock began to tick again.

Chapter 3

As time ticked on, those cute elementary children were speaking to my inner mother, and I felt ready to continue on the path to parenthood. A friend recommended an acupuncturist, so I went to get some regular fertility treatments. I bought fertility stones and put them near my bed. We tracked my ovulation with a predictor kit and timed sex to coincide with when I was most fertile. We even considered intrauterine insemination.

I was 38 when I got pregnant again and I was determined to make this one work. This time I did not hide it from my friends. I was ecstatic. It was a miracle. For the first time I wanted to tell people I was pregnant. I felt great for a couple of weeks— and then I started spotting.

I made an appointment with my OBGYN to be evaluated. I was excited and so hopeful to be pregnant again, but very anxious because of my previous miscarriages. The ultrasound showed a baby in my uterus and there was a heartbeat, but because of my history and "advanced age," she wanted me to take time off from work and stay in bed.

I was a bit panicked and asked her to double-check if there was a baby in my fallopian tube. She reassured me and confirmed that the baby was definitely in my uterus. Armed with hope and feeling safe, I went home and did what the doctor ordered.

After three weeks had passed, I started bleeding again and went in to see my doctor. This time there was no heartbeat. It was Halloween. I had miscarried again.

I felt defeated and weak. What was the problem? I was healthy and strong. I ate healthy foods and worked out. I was at a healthy weight. I didn't smoke. My husband was healthy and younger than me. I wasn't ready to quit, but I was starting to feel unclear as to what the future would hold. I was so lost in grief—once more I had failed myself and was completely heartbroken. The nurse gave me information to make an appointment for another HSG and a prescription for Doxycycline to start five days before. I went home to recover and to take some time to mourn before returning to work.

In a week's time I was ready to go back to work to occupy my mind and focus less on mourning; however, that did not happen. I started having extreme pain and could barely move. It felt like the first time I was pregnant and had a ruptured ectopic pregnancy. When I called my doctor, she informed me that there was only a 1 in 30,000 chance of a heterotopic pregnancy—a pregnancy complication with multiple fetuses, one intrauterine and the other ectopic. However, she suggested I go to the emergency room to be safe. If left untreated, it can cause internal bleeding and death for the woman, not to mention a miscarriage.

This jarring news sent me into a spiral; a mixture of fury and panic rolled into one. Had I not advocated for myself, I could have become another statistic. That scared and enraged me beyond measure. Had I known that there was an ectopic pregnancy at the start it could have been removed with over a 50% success rate of the intrauterine fetus surviving. I later learned that this type of pregnancy is actually much more common than I was told—1 in 7,000, a statistic that felt a lot more personal. My pain was too great to drive. Unable to reach my husband, I called my neighbor to help me get to emergency immediately.

When I arrived, the emergency team got me in quickly because my pain was so intense. I was so agitated and overwhelmed by a strange sense of déjà vu. I felt in my gut that I was reliving this whole experience—the pain, the fear, the anxiety of not knowing or trusting the medical system—and I was frightened that this might be a complication from the miscarriage. I had never been consulted to get a D&C, which some friends had told me about getting when they miscarried. The team did a blood and urine test and an ultrasound, which confirmed that I had an embryo in my fallopian tube. I had been pregnant with twins, but the second embryo did not make it to the uterus. It started growing in my fallopian tube and at just over twelve weeks, it burst the tube. Again, I found myself wondering what the outcome would have been had my OBGYN been more proactive. Would my pregnancy have survived? I went into surgery, and again, they could not save the pregnancy or the tube. I had no fallopian tubes left. I was consumed with anger, sadness, and an overwhelming feeling of how unfair everything was.

How would I get pregnant at this point?

I went home to recover and was given some medication for the pain. I had been emotionally messed up each time a miscarriage occurred, but this time was even harder, knowing that I could not get pregnant again. And now grieving two losses within a week. I was mourning the loss of the baby in my uterus and now the baby in my tube—the loss of my twins. I felt like I was living a nightmare rather than the dream I so desperately desired. I wanted to be a mom. Why was this happening to me? I had learned over the years about other's miscarriages, but it wasn't something that happened in my family. The unfairness made me so angry. I cried for hours as my husband held me in his arms. I felt lost and was experiencing a lack of purpose. I was in an existential crisis beyond any I had ever felt before.

Two weeks went by since the laparoscopic surgery for my ectopic pregnancy and I was still having pain. The emotional impact was so upsetting that it was on my mind often, but the pain in my body was agonizing. It hurt to move, and I couldn't even work out to help with the emotional or physical toll this had taken on me. I had a large area of bruising the size of a watermelon, lower pelvic pressure, neck and shoulder pain, it hurt to urinate, and was difficult to have a bowel movement. I was certain that with such massive bruising, which hadn't occurred during my first ectopic surgery, that I had been dropped. I demanded an MRI and a pelvic ultrasound to check for any internal issues. I was still carrying feelings of loss and anger, and I suppose I wanted to add blame into my grieving process. The staff and doctors assured me they didn't drop me. I showed no internal issues, so I let it go and continued my journey of grief and sorrow.

Grieving takes on so many stages and sometimes repeats them, so I asked the nurse if she knew of any resources to help me get through this. The nurse gave me information for a support group called Sharing Parents. This was a community of parents who had gone through a loss of a baby from conception through early infancy. My husband and I began attending the support group and found it very therapeutic. Even though Baby A, Sapphire, Sebastian, Angelica and Oliver would not exist in our life—it was helpful and comforting to know we weren't alone in our grief as we worked through it with others who had also experienced tremendous loss.

While my husband and I were navigating our grief and pain through a support group, my mother was also suffering. This final miscarriage had been extremely difficult on my mother as well. She felt like it was partly her fault and was so angry at God for letting this happen to her daughter. She had spent several years praying for me to have a baby. She knew how much I loved kids. While she was three months pregnant with me, she had an appendicitis attack and had to have an appendectomy. During that time, there was a drug given to women prior to surgery to prevent them from miscarrying. It wasn't until the early seventies that it was discovered to have some serious side effects for the developing unborn child.

But it wasn't until much later in my life that I would discover what the drug was. Throughout my life she had concerns regarding my health and encouraged me to exercise and eat healthy. My mom and I joined a gym when I was a sophomore in high school. This was the start of a lifestyle for me that would continue throughout my life. Inspired by my sister's career and passion for the Hippocrates Health Institute, I learned how to eat a healthy plant-based diet. I have continued to eat this way, although occasionally including dairy and eggs, and on rare occasions, fish.

I wasn't perfect in my healthy lifestyle; however, I was healthier for it. The next step was to figure out what was causing the infertility. I knew that artificial insemination would not be a viable option for me since I no longer had fallopian tubes, but another possibility could work for us—in vitro fertilization (IVF). I scheduled a hysteroscopy (HSC). In this procedure, the doctor used a telescope to check my uterus for any possible issues such as polyps, fibroids, or scar tissue— but everything seemed normal. I wanted to know if there were any options that we could explore other than IVF. As hard as it was to accept, this seemed to be the only path left if I wanted to give birth. Not the answer I was hoping for, though we were glad to hear that everything seemed normal, and I felt a sense of relief. Even so, beneath that relief, I couldn't shake the feeling that our journey to start a family might still hold more twists and turns on our road to parenthood. As new possibilities began to take shape in our minds, we found ourselves open to exploring whatever options the future might require.

Section 2

The Dream...Reimagined

My childhood dream of becoming a mother to 14 kids felt impossibly far away at this point. But I've learned we must take a different road to reach the dreams that light our path, even if that means changing direction from where we first began. There are bends, hills, and valleys I never could have seen at the journey's start. Still, as I moved forward—uncertain but persistent—I began to realize that the world of science and medicine might offer us a new gateway to motherhood, one I never expected but was suddenly willing to explore.

Chapter 4

This was the beginning of what would be several heart-breaking losses within a five-year span. It felt like one loss after another; the people I loved were being taken from me. My husband's brother, Andrew, passed away so suddenly from heart failure at only 29 years old in the spring of 2003. Then, just one year later, my dear childhood friend lost her son Arin in a car accident. He was only 15. These losses were devastating and gave me a new fear—how would a mom ever recover from such a heart-wrenching loss?

That same year, in October, my dear Aunt Atsuko lost her battle with cancer. This was a woman who had never been able to conceive and always wished she could have. Two years later, in October 2006, I lost my beloved mom to an unexpected brain aneurysm. Then, in April 2007, I received the devastating news that my lifelong friend Linda had taken her own life.

I had now experienced the pain of five miscarriages, two within this time frame, and the loss of five friends and family within five years. And during all this time I was going through my own quiet battle, trying to have a child. There were so many moments when it felt like joy and hope were just out of reach.

Adding to those feelings, I watched as friends around me celebrated pregnancies and hosted baby showers. I wanted so much to be genuinely happy for them—to support them and share in their excitement for this step in their lives. But honestly, sometimes it was just too much. I would make excuses and leave early, feeling pangs of jealousy and loss that I didn't know how to explain.

As a teacher, I sometimes struggled with feelings of frustration when I saw students whose needs were not being fully met at home. There were times I found myself longing to provide the care and support I believed they deserved, and it made me question fairness—not just with the crushed dreams of pregnancy, but how some people had children, yet failed to nurture. Recognizing these feelings helped me reflect on the complexities and challenges of parenting. I tried to remind myself that every family has unique challenges that aren't always visible. Compassion rather than judgment can be more comforting for all.

The grief of so many losses, together with the ongoing struggle of infertility, made it difficult for me to feel connected to my coworkers. Sometimes it felt like everyone else had a great life as I longed for starting my own family. Breaks and lunches in the staff room were especially tough. I often felt like an outsider listening to conversations about kids, dogs, and dinner recipes that didn't resonate with my own experience. I'd sometimes feel a sharp ache of loneliness and awkwardness, wishing so much that I could participate in their joyful banter. My sense of belonging seemed out of reach.

I refused to give up on my dreams of motherhood, and I knew I had to find peace with my losses in order to move forward. I knew there was another path to become a mom and I was ready to look into this route—in vitro fertilization

(IVF) was the journey to embark upon next. This appeared daunting, but I had met people who had success with this route, so I began researching to find out more.

I did not decide on this route lightly. In vitro fertilization was not cheap, and like many insurance companies, mine did not cover this expense. It would be costly, emotionally draining, and demand time and energy—yet it was the only way I could conceive and carry a biological child.

So the adventure began.

IVF is a complex series of procedures that included injecting myself with hormones. My health was important to me, and I liked doing things as natural as possible. This seemed out of character for me. I was scared at the thought of injecting a needle into my body. I was concerned about taking so many drugs, injecting hormones into my body, and the cost. I was reluctant to conceive a child in what seemed, to me, an unnatural way. A good friend of mine had just gone through the IVF process and had success. But this was more personal to decide to do it for myself.

Beyond the cost and concerns of introducing medications and hormones into my body, historically, there are ethical considerations surrounding IVF. It didn't cross my mind that this was a moral issue with my friend doing IVF, but I felt weird about the ethical dilemma of doing it myself. This was a new realization for me to even consider the morals around IVF. At this time, I wasn't a religious person, however, I had grown up in a religious home and science intervening with the miracle of life felt uneasy to me. Creating embryos outside of the womb seemed like playing God. And then there was the dilemma of donating or discarding unviable or unused embryos. What about the embryos that get donated to science for research? What were the ramifications of freezing the embryos and the likelihood of them surviving? I never thought I would even need to consider these ethical dilemmas. Then came the question—what if I got pregnant with multiples? How would I be able to handle another miscarriage or even raising quadruplets if they all survived? Putting a single embryo in my uterus would be more costly and less likely to be viable than if we put in three or four embryos. This was a most unsettling feeling. But after lots of research and conversations, we decided to go ahead with it.

I began reading up on IVF and the science surrounding it as well as the controversies. Once I learned how many years this practice had been in effect and understood the success rates, I began to feel more comfortable with the idea. After all, God did create humans and gave us the ability to become scientists. I likened discarding unviable embryos to miscarriage and decided I could always donate any unused embryos to another couple who couldn't conceive without medical intervention. After lots of research and conversations, we decided to go ahead with it.

Finding a practice that provided IVF took some investigating. This took countless hours of tireless research and endless phone calls. Luckily having the Internet made this a bit easier. I researched places near and far. I felt reluctant to travel too far, so we decided to stay near home for the convenience. After narrowing it down to four places near us, we went to visit the clinics and interview the doctors. These interviews helped us to verify questions I had already researched and to get a feel for each environment. I wanted to work with staff and doctors that had a good "bedside manner" because I knew this was going to be a difficult and emotional experience. I wanted to feel at ease.

Once we found the place where we felt comfortable, the next step was to begin an intense regimen of prerequisite fertility testing. Both my husband and I had to do a bunch of tests. The extensive testing for us was quite tedious and all expenses were out of pocket. But the dream was worth the costs. All the testing had to be done before we would be approved to continue with IVF. This could end positively and encourage awareness, or could result in an ego death for either or both of us. Fortunately, everything was in the normal range, and no positive cultures. Daunting, but a relief. We were good to go. I decided to try IVF because I truly hoped it would work, even though I knew there were no guarantees. Still, I felt in my heart that I had to give it a chance, so that no matter what happened, I wouldn't look back with regrets for not having tried... The IVF process could begin. Thank the Universe!

Drugs in excess were about to fill my body—a portion in pill form, some as suppositories, and a fair amount of subcutaneous (injected under the skin) or intramuscularly (into the muscle): Desogen; (birth control pills); prenatal vitamins; Gonal-F (subcutaneous), a follicle stimulating hormone (FSH); Luveris (subcutaneous), a follicle stimulating hormone (FSH); Ovidrel (subcutaneous) to ripen follicles containing eggs and trigger ovulation; a human chorionic gonadotropin (hCG);

Lupron (subcutaneous), a luteinizing hormone-releasing hormone (LHRH); Estradiol (subcutaneous); Methylprednisolone (subcutaneous) to prepare the endometrium for implantation; aspirin to assist in blood flow to the implantation site; Erythromycin, an antibiotic to treat a suspected or possible bacterial infection that may occur before or during an IVF cycle; Doxycycline, used to help control bacteria and reduce the risk of infection; Progesterone in oil (injectable) to thicken the endometrial lining and help it to implant the fertilized egg; and an anesthetic for sedation during egg retrieval.

Once I accepted the idea of flooding my body with IVF meds, next in line was figuring out how to afford the IVF drugs. The medications were more expensive in the United States (it's not recommended to purchase them abroad due to concerns with quality and legitimacy) but purchasing them outside the country meant I could buy them at a much better price. This research took a bit longer. I wanted to be sure if I went out of country, I was getting legitimate IVF drugs. After some due diligence, I made the decision to save a couple thousand dollars and order them out of country. I found a reputable pharmacy in London and placed my order online.

I was ecstatic when the package finally arrived, though I felt quite nervous about starting the injections. I wasn't afraid of needles. In fact, I am the person who doesn't look away when the nurse takes my blood or gives me a shot. I was just nervous about giving *myself* a shot. It wasn't like I had to find a vein since the injections were subcutaneous (under the skin). But the idea of sticking a needle into myself seemed foreign. My mind was flooded with thoughts about the journey I was about to embark on. I was feeling thrilled that I was alive in a time when this was even possible. Then again, I was scared about the side effects. And even a bit worried that the drugs I purchased would not work. So many emotions—excitement, fear, and anxiety—all intertwined. What would this do to my overall health in the future? We are all so unique, who could tell? But here I was, about to shoot myself up with various hormones. However, the result could be my dream of becoming a mother. And that thought brought me joy.

Before I even began the injections, waves of grief would wash over me. I found myself thinking about all the loss I had already been through—the pain of the miscarriages, each one so difficult in its own way. On top of that, I was still carrying the loss of loved ones, especially the fresh loss of my mom, whose absence was the hardest of all to bear. She had always been my biggest cheerleader, my constant source of comfort and support. Continuing this journey without her beside me made everything feel so much heavier and more daunting. But I did have my dad and my sisters to cheer me on now, and they were there for me whenever I needed comfort and support. The memories of my lost loved ones and the love of my family would have to be the tender mercies through this journey.

Despite the support I had from familiar faces, everything still felt strangely fragile. My older sister who'd always embraced all things natural—she'd even had six children, all born at home—flew from Maine to California to be with me. She brought her four youngest, and together they watched as I stuck needles into my belly and thighs every day. Their presence should have made everything feel normal, and in some ways, it did. But their wide-eyed curiosity, the contrast between their easy laughter and my trembling hands, made my choices stand out—unconventional, uncertain, yet necessary. The acceptance they gave me was gentle and real, though underneath it all, I felt a current of anxiety. I was stepping into the unknown, hoping this path that was so different than my sister's would lead me toward my dream.

Chapter 5

Preparation. Poked. Prodded. The beginning of the relentless procedures and tests that encompassed my journey to motherhood. A taxing series of blood draws, injections, and still more procedures. All the testing and questions made me feel exposed and raw, like there was no part of me that wasn't being examined or judged. This is IVF.

There are several stages to the in vitro fertilization process. These are the ones I experienced.

Preparation

The first phase is the preparation. This is where the body is prepped for treatment. In this stage both my husband and I had to undergo testing to check for any underlying causes of infertility. All this testing felt like being caught in an endless experiment—so many blood draws, peeing in cups, ultrasounds, questions, and pokes. Some days, I felt less like a patient and more like a lab rat, subjected to endless tests—my life boiled down to numbers and timing. It's all so intense, and sometimes the emotional weight—fear, hope, vulnerability—hits harder than the physical stuff.

The waiting was torture—always bracing myself for news, wondering if these tests would bring answers or just more confusion. There was this fear of the unknown that followed me, making it all feel more overwhelming. Though the good news afterwards was reassuring, and I felt relief and reenergized to go on to the next stage.

After enduring all the prep work, my body was forced into suppression of my menstrual cycle using birth control pills, which felt seemingly contrary given the journey I was embarking on. The birth control pills help to temporarily suppress the hormone production, preventing spontaneous ovulation by halting the ovaries from developing follicles on their own, and to keep the risk of developing ovarian cysts at bay. I felt that was a good thing to not have happen. Not to mention the regulation of the cycle to control the timing as to better schedule the treatments for IVF. This was a definite benefit considering the magnitude of this itinerary, taking anywhere from 10 to 21 days before starting the follicle stimulating hormones (FSH). The trepidation of injecting myself with needles then begins.

Ovarian Stimulation

Egg production. Never in my dream did I ever imagine I'd be so invested in the number of eggs my body could create. Being a woman around forty made it less likely I would produce a lot. However, I tried to stay focused on my health-age rather than my chronological-age. Optimism helped put me in the eye of the storm.

I think the craziest part of this hormone consumption was the shots in the buttocks. I was fearful of the longer needle, and I couldn't see where it was going. The first injection was done by my husband, but I also had to give myself shots during my lunch hour at work. This was incredibly weird. I would go into the bathroom and lock the door to give myself the shot in my upper butt. This was quite challenging. I felt like I was shooting for the bullseye, blindfolded. Not easy at first, but it got simpler.

Jabbed. Punctured. Jabbed. Punctured.

Intravenous, pills, and suppositories.

Blood drawn for multiple lab testing.

Why was I doing this to my body? All just to get pregnant, with no guarantee that I would.

I was beginning to feel like I was drowning in appointments, information, hormones, and decisions. It was hard to keep up, and sometimes I just wanted to hide under a rock.

Retrieval

Push forward to the third stage, retrieval. During this phase, I was given anesthesia before injecting the long needle into my vagina. I was told that it was to help me relax and to not feel any pain. It worked. I didn't feel anything. I was relaxed and ready to gather the eggs from my ovaries.

The doctor was able to retrieve 23 eggs, of which five were abnormal, two showed no evidence of culture (non-viable), and one was immature. I was so thrilled when I learned that I was so prosperous! The abnormal and immature eggs were discarded; you can't fertilize a bad egg. I had 15 good eggs. This was considered a success. I will say that this seemed so promising, and I was feeling very fortunate that I had so many eggs to work with. I was told that at my age, 39, I would be lucky to get about 10 eggs, yet I produced 23—albeit only 15 were viable. Still, this was above the average, and I felt quite hopeful that we would be able to conceive at least one. Good news! What's next?

Fertilization

After the eggs were retrieved, the good ones were put into glass petri dishes immediately. Then fertilized with the capacitated sperm. Within three to five days, the fertilized eggs develop into the next phase. Embryo development here we come. I felt like I was at a casino playing craps—though these stakes were priceless.

Parts of me harvested. Fertilized in a petri dish. Not unlike high school science class. But here a grade wasn't at risk—a human life was.

Embryo Development

Next stage—the blastocyst, the moment when a fertilized egg splits and begins its 3-5 day journey to become both an embryo and a placenta. This is one of the coolest and most mind-blowing events in human biology. At least I think so. Although not all will reach the blastocyst stage, where they are considered viable for this uterus transfer. In my case, 12 reached the blastocyst stage; however, not all twelve could be transferred. That would be madness. Imagine if they all took? Gives a whole new meaning to *Cheaper by the Dozen*.

Embryo Transfer

The final stage of IVF—embryo transfer and the hope for implantation. The moment where science, hope, and love all converged in my heart. Everything felt so surreal. After thoughtful discussions with the medical team and among ourselves, we decided to transfer three embryos and freeze the rest.

Within minutes, the tiniest bundle of hope was gingerly placed into my womb, and I could barely believe this was happening to me. My mind began racing with excitement, fear, and overwhelming hope. Lying there after the transfer, I couldn't help but imagine those little embryos searching for a home on my uterine wall, wanting so much for at least one of them to settle in and grow into my sweet bundle of joy. Feeling vulnerable, but so full of possibility—and then it dawned on me—there is the chance that more than one can attach and continue to grow into a fetus. Then it hit hard—the cognitive dissonance—a panicked feeling of all three embryos attaching, followed by the comfort of what a blessing it would be to have three in one try. So many emotions in such a short time. More than anything, I just wanted to let myself believe that a new chapter could be beginning right now. The longest part of this phase was now waiting for eleven days for the blood test to determine if the pregnancy is positive. Eleven days. Probably the longest eleven days of my life up until this point in my life.

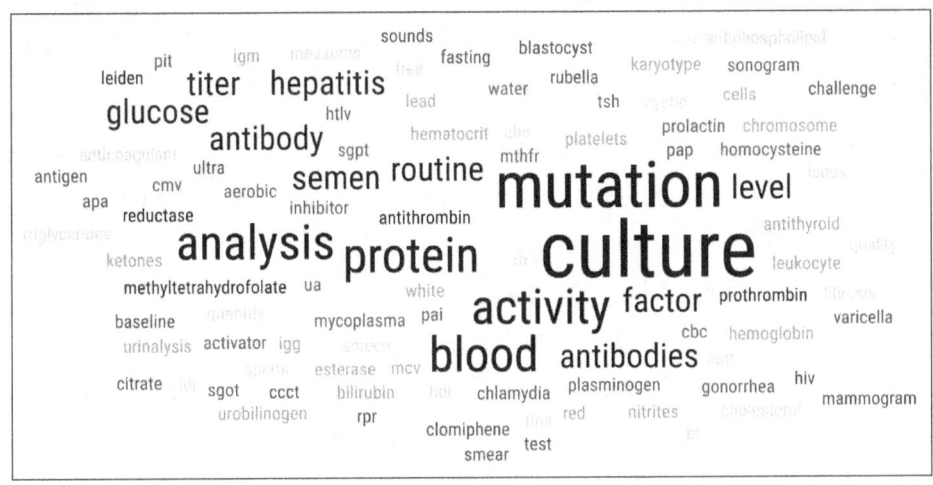

Chapter 6

I was not exactly a religious person, nor did I pray. But I unwittingly asked my friends and family to do so by asking for their positive thoughts. At the end of the eleven days, I had my pregnancy blood test done and was told that my human chorionic gonadotropin (hCG) level was high enough to show a positive pregnancy. I was elated and my heart was soaring, yet I was terrified at the same time.

I knew that I would redo the blood test in two more days to determine if the hCG levels were rising. The losses I had endured came rushing back and triggered a moment of fear. I took some deep breaths and told myself to stay positive, that the levels would be rising. It was hard not to be nervous having had so many letdowns in the past. I was secretly preparing for another loss. I didn't think of it as being optimistic or pessimistic, just realistic. I could see that I was just building up my defenses. It was so difficult for me to be in a vulnerable position once again. I just wanted to hide from the pain that kept creeping back from the losses.

Two days later, I took another test to see if my levels were getting higher. I eagerly awaited the results. I kept vigil by my phone—holding my breath, heart in my throat. So much was riding on this test, I felt I would collapse under the pressure of my hope and my fear. I could feel the excitement creating a tingling sensation from within. The hopeful feeling of living my dream. The realization that I would finally be a mother. Unsure what the results would be. The tumultuous mind games of it not happening and the gut-wrenching disappointment that would follow. It was an emotional storm. High, low, up, and down. The unknown can be absolutely terrifying—and, at this point in my journey, it truly was. Every step forward felt like stepping off a cliff into total darkness. I was overwhelmed by uncertainty, anxiety swirling in my stomach, along with tightness in my chest. The fear was real, and it consumed me entirely.

Later that day, the call I was both anticipating and dreading finally came. My hCG level was dropping, and it appeared I had lost the pregnancy. I was crushed. My energy and hope plummeted until I remembered I still had nine embryos frozen. All hope was not lost, but I was feeling pretty low over this news. I will admit that when I got off the phone, I cried quite a bit. How was this fair? I threw the phone across the room.

Grief ripped through my body like a scream, flooding me with out-of-character thoughts booming through my mind—blame, resentment, disbelief. Haunted by how others' unhealthy choices somehow still granted them the dream I yearned for most: the fragile, aching hope of having a child.

Two months later, after slowly untangling those heavy emotions, we felt a gentle hope rising between us. When my next cycle came, we decided, with a mixture of courage and longing, to try again. No luck. Then again after my next period. Again, a failure. This time I decided to wait another three months.

It was my 40th birthday when I got the news that the last of my frozen embryos that had been implanted was not showing hCG levels rising. My birthday. A day that's supposed to be filled with joy and celebration was marred by the devastation of more failed attempts. Instead of happiness, I found myself sitting with deep grief and disappointment, feeling like my dreams of becoming a mother were moving further and further away. Even this day wasn't safe from the heaviness that had settled around me. The heartache was impossible to ignore, and all I could do was mourn the loss of hope, even on the day that should have been special. Happy birthday to me. What a letdown of a birthday. I was now 40, and had miscarried five times and had four failed attempts at in vitro fertilization. I felt defeated and old. If I was old at 35 for having children, now I was ancient. The grief consumed me, my age defying my desire. What could I do to stop this heartache? I opted to drown my sorrows by drinking, something to numb the pain. A very low moment indeed.

Another two months went by when we decided to give it another shot. Despite the past failures, we still had hope. The clock kept ticking and we wanted to nurture the spark. We began the cycle anew—creating another round of eggs and embryos—trusting that among them, one might grow into the miracle we longed for. By midsummer, we had another successful harvest. Not as bountiful as the first, but nevertheless, we were ecstatic that we had viable embryos.

We held close the few precious embryos we had—each one full of silent hope. With hopeful hands and silent strength, we prepared ourselves to try once more, letting faith lead us once again into the unknown, wishing with all our heart that this would be the moment our long-awaited dream would finally take root. But the pregnancy was negative. Once again, the mournful sigh of failure. Not just of the loss of a pregnancy, but of time, energy, hope, and the future we had envisioned.

That same month, my sister Becky wrote a letter to the fertility center in regard to any fertilized eggs that remain in case of our death. It was to inform them that she would take possession of them in the event that death occurred. I was deeply moved and comforted by my sister's wish to carry forward our hope, feeling an indescribable gratitude knowing our family's love could give these tiny possibilities another chance—even if we could not. At the time, it didn't even occur to me that this would become such a controversial thing in about 20 years with the abolishment of Roe vs. Wade. Eggs would typically be destroyed otherwise.

We tried in the fall, and again a failure. We had three frozen embryos left and waited until the following spring to try again. I was certain that if there was a God, this was just a test in patience and that this time, it would be successful. I was persistent to get this far. For sure my perseverance would be rewarded. But success was not in the cards for me. Once again, the IVF attempt had failed.

The overwhelming disappointment was too much for me to bear. How could I keep going? I tried to shift my mindset beyond being a parent, searching for the benefits of being childless. Maybe it was the rewards of being a DINK (double income no kids). Maybe the ability to go out without needing to find a babysitter or traveling more easily. We would save money for other dreams and aspirations.

However, the lingering need to be a mother was not going away anytime soon. I wanted that dream to become a reality. I needed that dream to become a reality. For reasons unknown, IVF was not working for us, and the expense was becoming too great for uncertainty. What was left? We decided to meet with the infertility specialist at the clinic to discuss next steps.

Surrogacy was now on the table. This was not an easy discussion. I really wanted to have the experience of carrying a baby full-term, giving birth, and nursing. Though that was not a possibility, this option could give us a baby that would be our bloodline. My husband wanted the surrogate to be local. My sister, who had successfully given birth to six children (all home births and healthy), offered to be our surrogate. I trusted this option and was extremely grateful that she was willing to carry our child. The boundless depth of her love was incredibly touching. But there were two issues. The first being she lived in Maine, not California, and the other was she was now forty-nine years old. My husband did not like the distance factor and the doctors said she was too old.

All hope was not lost; my 25-year-old niece lived nearby and gave us a glimmer of peace—she offered to be our surrogate. The distance was much closer and was a better option because of age. Unfortunately, our doctor was not so supportive of this because she had never given birth. At that point I felt defeated. I had been so thrilled that she was willing to do this great sacrifice for us out of love, and the doctor had said no.

The only option left for surrogacy would be to use a stranger. After all the heartbreak I had already endured—each grief inscribing its weight upon my soul—I could not bring myself to trust a stranger with our child. The thought of taking that risk felt too sharp, too uncertain. My heart, already bruised by miscarriage and IVF, wasn't ready or willing to brave another unknown. What if she became attached and refused to surrender the baby? The amount of loss we had endured was too great to risk any more sorrow. I could conceive of a surrogate that we knew, but not a stranger. This was just too unimaginable for me to wrap my head around. A boundary I could not cross.

The decision for surrogacy was now null and void.

Chapter 7

Infertility forced me to confront so many kinds of absence. And the one woven through all those failed attempts of becoming a mom was the unimaginable loss of my mom—a pain that touched everything that came after. I recall the day I received a phone call from my sister, Bonnie, that my mom had fallen due to a brain aneurism and was in the hospital. The prognosis did not look good. The doctors had determined that she had suffered severe brain damage. I was teaching my seventh-grade math class when I received the call. I dropped everything, frantically purchasing a ticket for the next flight to Portland. When I arrived, my brother-in-law picked me up and drove me to the hospital where my mom had been admitted earlier. No sooner had I arrived, I heard the inconceivable—the aneurysm had ruptured. She was alive and on life support, but she was brain dead. They had her on a ventilator but she was unresponsive. The doctors showed me the brain scans—it was a massive hemorrhage. She could be kept alive, but she would not be herself. There was an overwhelming helplessness, standing on the edge of a goodbye that I could not yet fully say.

For a while, I felt nothing—just a stunned emptiness, as if the world had gone silent around me. After spending a few hours with my mother and my sister, I finally was ready to let go, knowing she had a directive that she did not want to be kept alive on a ventilator. I had accepted that this was the fate to be handed down to us. I knew this was the last gift I could give her: release from pain, though it broke my heart to let go.

We were asked if we wanted to paint her hand and make handprints by which to remember her. I thought this was strange, but I was up for it. We giggled a bit while doing this. I wondered if my mom had any awareness of what was happening. I think she would have giggled too if she could.

It was nearly the end of the day. I asked if we could wait to take her off life support until after midnight so her death would be Friday the 13th. My sense of humor can be a bit morbid in difficult moments. I suppose it helps me cope when life feels heavy and surreal. I was in a state of disbelief that I was about to lose my mother. I felt so incredibly sad that I had not been able to see her be a grandparent to my kids. Losing my ability to birth children and my mother in the same year left me hollowed out by double grief—two futures stolen at once, leaving an ache where hope and love had lived.

When we made the difficult decision to withdraw the life support treatment, we held her until she was no longer warm. This moment was exceptionally surreal. This was the woman who gave us life and now we were ending hers. I only felt comfort in knowing that this was the gift she had requested in her lucid days. With heavy hearts, we drew the sheet gently over her face, a final act of tenderness, now that all breath and warmth had gone. Tears rolled down my cheeks.

With tears in my eyes and love overflowing in my heart, we stepped outside my mother's hospital room into a world that felt painfully empty, yet full of her quiet presence. We walked quietly, carrying our grief in every step as we left the hospital, and with despair clouding our hearts, drove to a nearby restaurant. It was 2:00 a.m. and the world outside felt strangely quiet and unchanged. We had not eaten for a while, and hunger was gnawing at us and sleep was impossible in the shadow of our despair. The drive was hauntingly silent—the most surreal experience had just unfolded, leaving me feeling as if I were caught in a moment outside reality. Just when things seemed dark, a sense of peace began to emerge, a sweet reminder that even in the midst of sorrow, a silver lining nudged me, and I felt a glimmer of joy to have been with her when she died, and to have shared this experience with my sister and dear friend, Bonnie. I now look back and relish the tender mercy in this.

Even as we tried to hold ourselves together beneath the weight of our raw grief, we were reminded there was a funeral and memorial service that needed to be arranged. A couple days later we were at my mom's apartment going through her things, and I came across the funeral service program of her father and noticed that he had also died on October 13th. Even more interesting, it was on a Friday that year, 1978, as well. What an interesting world it can be.

My mother, always thinking ahead, had set up her burial years before she passed, so we had a plot and tombstone waiting. She had even paid for her own cremation. In the depths of our sadness, her planning felt like one last embrace, her love shining through every detail. Even in her absence she was caring for us, trying to cushion our loss as only she could. So organized and helpful in a time of sorrow. Love that woman—her kindness and forethought will stay with us forever.

Bonnie bravely took on the task of calling relatives and friends, sharing the news of Mom's passing with care and compassion—inviting people to the service and selecting the right music. Every song we considered became a testament of the love she shared with us and the lasting imprint she left behind. In those melodies, we hoped to find a sense of peace and connection in our time of grief.

As I wrote the eulogy and created the program for my mother's service, I found myself sifting through a lifetime of memories—cherished moments, quiet laughter, and feeling the warmth of her presence. Each story I included, every detail in the program, was a way of honoring the life she lived and the love she gave so freely.

We invited everyone to bring a potluck dish—both to make it easier on us and to pay tribute to a well-loved tradition from her days in the Methodist Church, where we so often gathered and shared meals together. It felt comforting and fitting to remember her in a way that reflected the warmth and togetherness she always enjoyed.

While we were at the crematorium, I found myself wanting to understand more about what happens, so as a way to cope with my grief, I let my morbid curiosity creep in. I asked to have the process explained to me in detail. Hearing the scientific aspects of it was unexpectedly fascinating and helped me find a sense of peace with it all. He delicately conversated with me, telling me basically that since our bodies are mostly water, most of our body dissipates in the heat while what is left are finely broken pieces of bone, or ashes.

Once the formalities were finally over, an even heavier sadness hit me. The reality struck hard. I would never have kids who would know their grandmother—her warm hugs, her laughter, her wise stories, the way she could make even the smallest things feel special. The anger then gripped me, sharp and relentless. Why did she have to die? Why did she have to go before I could give her grandkids, before I could introduce my future to my past?

When I thought about it, the grief grew in all directions. Losing babies is losing your dreams for the future; losing your mom is losing where I came from and the shared history of days gone by. This was too much for me to let in, but I knew I needed to grieve, no matter how much it hurt.

Suddenly, spirituality, to which I hadn't paid much attention, felt like a path I needed to follow. Something that might help me make sense of this suffering or at least keep me moving when the world felt exceedingly empty. In that moment I realized I was reaching, desperately, for something bigger than myself, some way to cherish the memories that slipped away and the dreams that never came true.

Section 3

Opening Doors: Finding Family in Unexpected Places

As I opened myself to new possibilities, I began to find hope and the chance for connection and belonging in ways I never expected. Now, as I take my first steps down the path toward adoption, I feel a tender growing sense of love in my heart.

Chapter 8

After a few lonely months had gone by, I slowly, almost without noticing, began to feel light again—seeking something new that life might have in store for me. I had been trying to get comfortable with the idea of not being a parent. But there was still that nudge deep inside my soul, a longing to have children that I could nurture outside the classroom. I had considered the possibility of becoming a foster parent, but that didn't quite fill my desire to raise a child of my own. Adoption scared me, but I wondered if that could work—if I were to adopt an infant, maybe that would be enough. Still, the thoughts in my head wouldn't stop swirling, caught in a conflicted and anxious loop.

And then one day, a friend of mine was listening to me lament over where my life might take me, and she told me if she were in my shoes, she would probably adopt. In my early twenties the thought of adoption had now and then crossed my mind; however, after marriage, I was overtaken by the excitement of imagining a little one who might have my smile or my husband's curly red hair—a tiny reflection of both of us and all our dreams intertwined. Could adoption be my path? Could I fully love a child I haven't carried for nine months who may not look like me? Would it matter? Why not? The thought of adoption stayed with me, and I could viscerally feel this pulsing through my body, and I began investigating.

As I began exploring the world of adoption, my heart buzzed with anticipation and a twinge of uncertainty. There were so many different ways forward and the possibilities felt thrilling and just a little overwhelming.

I had already spent about $30,000 on IVF and thought a foster adoption could be an affordable route. Foster adoption could be a chance to open my heart and home to a child in need. This process involves legally adopting a child who was placed in foster care because their family was unable to care for them, often due to abuse or neglect. Unlike traditional adoption, foster adoption typically involves children who may be older and have experienced trauma or instability.

Part of me ached with doubt, questioning if I had the strength or the heart for this. I nervously delved into foster adoption through the state. I found this route could take years and had no guarantees. Could I truly open myself to love and loss all over again? I talked with a few people who had tried this and heard several stories about the birth parents coming back, either before or after a final adoption, and receiving custody. Having dealt with so much loss, I felt too anxious with this path. I would be completely devastated if I adopted a child, fell in love, and then had them taken from me by the courts. It would shatter me.

The idea of adoption began to create some anxiety in my mind, and so many questions. What if I couldn't love this child as much as my own birth child? What if I didn't connect with the child and decided to give them back? I worried that somehow my heart wouldn't know how to make that connection—that love might feel forced or incomplete, or that I'd always be aware of the difference. It was an honest fear that kept circling in my mind. I had heard of adoptive parents doing this, and it filled me with dread. The thought of turning a child away, after giving them the hope of a family, felt unthinkable—like a wound to both their heart and mine. The thoughts and questions didn't ease up. What if the child didn't love me? This would be heart-wrenching, stirring up doubts about whether I could be enough. What if? What if? What if? The what if game continued in my head until I realized the truth. My childhood dream was simply to be a mom; it never had anything to do with giving birth. All I longed for was the chance to love and nurture a child, and adoption was the only way this dream could finally come true.

With that dream in my heart, the next step was to look into adoption through the state—a new research project that opened yet another chapter in my journey. Adopting through the state was almost completely funded by state or local government. There were many children available for adoption whose biological parents had their rights termi-nated. The reality was that many of these kids were older and I really wanted an infant. Also, many of the older kids had psychological trauma. Many of the infants had disabil-ities because they were born with prenatal substance exposure or had fetal alcohol syndrome. Given the trauma and sadness I experienced, I had to acknowledge the limits of what I could handle, what I could offer. Over the years I had worked with several kids who had various disabilities and trauma. I loved these kids and would do anything for them. But I was not sure I could be a parent to them. While I was in awe of people who could adopt and foster children with severe challenges, I had to be honest with myself about what would be right for me—I was longing for a baby who had a strong start physically and emotionally. So, this wasn't a path I wanted to take either.

After learning about state adoption, I began to explore the possibilities of private adoption, curious about what this path could offer. This was much more expensive. In 2007 the cost ranged from $25,000 to $60,000, and sometimes even more, depending on the health insurance of the birth mother, attorney fees, adoption agency (or if you go through several agencies), and travel expenses. This seemed like a safer route; however, I again found stories of the birth parent backing out after giving birth or even months later, wanting their baby back and getting the child back. More anxiety and more risk ensued in my mind.

I continued my research for private adoption and discovered that the adoptive parents had to build a profile to try to sell themselves as the prospective parents. The birth parent would then go through these portfolios and choose the adoptive parents for their baby. This whole process seemed very intimidating. The thoughts started rushing through my head in an endless loop.

Why would they choose us?

What if there was always someone better?

What if it took years before we were chosen?

With private adoption came other choices to consider. Was it going to be an open or closed adoption? In an open adoption the adoptive parents continue a relationship with the birth parent(s) throughout the child's life. A closed adoption, however, would prevent the birth parent(s) and the adoptive parents from having knowledge of one another—no personal information or contact whatsoever. The idea of a closed adoption made me uncomfortable, knowing that my child might have questions and I would not be able to answer. The prospect of an open adoption made me anxious. I worried about confusing roles and boundaries. Would I be able to share parenting? Some adoptions could be semi-closed where the adoptive parents send updates to the birth parent(s), but there is no relationship with the birth child, or variations on this. While other semi-closed adoptions would allow medical records/history of the birth family to be released to the adoptive parents. I have a friend who gave her birth child up for adoption and had an open relationship with the child and adoptive family. It felt overwhelming to sort through all the possibilities. I was uncertain about how much secrecy or openness would truly be right for my family and my future child.

Another discussion point is whether or not to have documents sealed until the adopted child is eighteen and can decide for themselves if they want to seek a meeting or relationship with their birth family. This gave me a sense of relief—I liked the idea that they would have the power to decide for themselves, in their own time, if and when they wanted to seek out their birth family. Or maybe for a health emergency to get family history information. This could be lifesaving. I know if I were the adoptee, I would want this option. This gave me peace and solace in this colossal and difficult decision-making process.

At this time, I was reverberating more thoughts of loss. What if the child hates me and wants to go find their birth parents or even go back to them and leave me stranded without my baby. I could not fathom losing my child. My feelings of inadequacy were being triggered by this interference in my head about being a failure in giving birth and then again in parenthood. It seemed hard to give in to the thought of this happening. An open adoption was way too difficult to imagine. What if the child's birth parent ended up being the child's favorite parent. This thought stung deeply—after so much loss, the idea that my child might turn to their birth parent as their preferred parent brought a wave of fear and sadness. I worried about being replaced, as if my love would not be enough. It was a painful insecurity, one that made my heart ache at the possibility of yet another loss—this time of the bond I so desperately hoped to build.

Then there was the question of whether the birth mother had twins. Would that be a deal breaker? Maybe not. My heart leaned toward the sweet notion of giving two little ones the chance to grow up, side by side. If that were even an option. How could I pass this option up, considering my final natural pregnancy was twins—albeit heterotopic. This would be a miracle. Could I be this lucky? The mind goes on and on...

I just couldn't get over the fear of a birth parent changing their mind and the loss of yet another child. I felt bothered by the idea of putting together a portfolio for a parent choosing adoption for their child and being judged by them. It was hard to accept that the chance to become a parent depended on being chosen by someone who didn't really even know me. I had struggled for so many years to have a child, and ultimately, it all came down to the decision of a woman who felt she couldn't raise her baby herself. In what universe was this fair? I was struggling so hard to accept the idea of private adoption and entangling in duality. Was I being punished for something? Was this the universe telling me that I am not mommy material?

Both intellectually and emotionally, I knew that if I were in the position of having to place my own baby for adoption, it would be an incredibly difficult and painful decision to make. Having a choice in who raises this child I created would be a comfort and reassure me that my child would be well taken care of. But I was the adoptive parent with a heavy suitcase, psychological baggage, and wasn't willing to concede.

Private adoption was not for me.

Why couldn't I be more open and flexible to adoption? I felt selfish when I talked about wanting a healthy child that would only know us as their parents, but that's exactly what I wanted. I had too many contradicting thoughts shooting through my mind—so many mixed feelings about going through private adoption. There was a nagging feeling of uncertainty and self-questioning whether I was choosing the right path. The emotional weight of it all left me feeling exhausted. My body was not willing to concede.

Was there another option I could explore? Maybe international adoption was the right path I could consider, one that might offer a different set of possibilities. This was the moment I realized that I wanted a healthy baby. What that child looked like or from where it came were no longer of concern. I could raise a child from another country. I had been teaching English language learners from many parts of the globe and children of various races for over ten years. I enjoyed being around other cultures and traveling. Learning was one of my favorite things to do. It could be exciting to learn about another culture and teach my child about their culture. It could be a life of adventure and growth. I was ready to dive into learning about international adoption and the different countries from which to choose.

I felt an immense thrill in my bones resonating as we began this next part of our adoption journey.

Chapter 9

After so much heartache and loss, I finally felt a shift toward hope—a hope that began to open the possibility of an exciting, though unfamiliar path. International adoption was something outside my circle of friends and family, and it all felt brand new to me. I had seen glimpses of international adoption in the news, including stories of celebrities who had chosen that road—which made it seem intriguing, yet intimidating. My worldview was about to be widened through this exploration of adopting internationally.

My husband and I had several countries to learn about that allowed international adoption. In 2007, the countries that were most commonly available for international adoption were Bulgaria, China, Colombia, Ethiopia, Guatemala, India, Romania, Russia, South Korea, Ukraine, and Vietnam. Most of these countries had signed the Hague Convention, an international agreement intended to safeguard intercountry adoptions. Vietnam was the only one of these countries that had not signed the agreement. Although the United States had signed it in 1994, it didn't officially go into effect until April 1, 2008.

The preamble for the Hague Adoption Convention can be summarized as: Children thrive in loving, happy, and supportive families. Wherever possible, efforts are made to keep children with their birth parents. If that's not possible, intercountry adoption may provide the chance for a permanent family. All adoptions are guided by the child's best interests, with strict protection of their rights (in accordance with the United Nations Convention on the Rights of the Child) and international standards to prevent child trafficking and ensure safe, ethical placement.

Having familiarized myself with the international agreements that guide adoption, I was eager to see how these principles would shape my journey and the choices available when it came to selecting a country. To learn more, I went to several adoption agencies in the area to gather information on their programs, hoping to find the right fit. I wanted to know about the process, length of process, cost, age requirements, in country orphanages, and cultural history.

Given that my husband and I are both Caucasian, the possibility of adopting a child that looked like us was intriguing. Then people wouldn't question if our child was adopted, to help minimize any potential awkwardness for the child as they adjust to our family and the culture of the United States—although this was by no means a requirement for us.

Russia's adoption process would take about 1-2 years and require multiple trips to the country. The amount of time in country ranged from 2-6 weeks, depending on any issues that might arise. Russia was the most expensive, at nearly $50,000 in total cost.

Bulgaria could take anywhere from 1-5 years. Total cost was approximately $25,000 to $30,000. But five years was too long of a wait to gamble with for us.

Ukraine adoptions generally took 12-18 months, and you had to choose your child when you visited the orphanage. Time spent in country was typically 2-3 weeks. The average cost was about $25,000.

Generally, Guatemala adoptions took up to 18 months; 1-4 weeks in country, and up to three trips. The price range was between $25,000 and $30,000.

South Korea took 18-24 months to complete an adoption, and adoptive parents had the option of traveling or hiring an escort to bring the baby to the U.S.A. If one traveled there, it would be a two-week maximum trip. South Korea came in second for most expensive, at close to $40,000.

China was taking up to 3-6 years and time in country was three weeks or less. The price was lower at around $25,000, but the wait was just too long for us to consider.

Ethiopia's adoption timeline was 12-24 months, two trips, and two weeks or less in country. The cost ranged from about $18,000 to $22,000.

Vietnam's adoption process took 12-24 months and one trip to Vietnam that lasted two to three weeks. Total cost from $25,000 to $30,000.

Adopting special needs kids would have been a faster and less expensive process. Although, I knew in my heart that I might not be the right person to provide the level of care and support that such a child deserves. As much as I admire families who are able to open their hearts in that way, my husband and I felt that adopting an infant without those challenges would be the best fit for us.

Sorting through all the costs and requirements for each country's international adoption process was both exciting and a little ironic. While I was full of hope about starting a family, I couldn't help but notice how easily the experience could feel transactional—with so many details to compare and consider, the joyful anticipation sometimes mingled with the practical realities of paperwork and checklists. At times, the sheer volume of information left my head spinning, making me wonder how something so heartfelt could also feel so complicated.

Through all the research, questions, and interviews of adoptive parents, it was clear that Vietnam fit our criteria best. I was drawn to Vietnam, especially since all the families we interviewed spoke highly of how professional and smooth the adoption process was. Another bonus was the cost was more affordable at around $25,000 to $30,000. Vietnam was a one-trip excursion that would give us some time in country to get a feel for the culture without being there too long. This would cut down on some of the time and cost. On top of that, the country's rich history seemed especially intriguing since my husband's father had spent several years in Vietnam during the war and never discussed it. Additionally, we had not heard any horror stories of Vietnam adoptions like we had about Russia, Ukraine, and Bulgaria.

We decided that the sex of the baby was not important so this would help with getting a referral, being matched with a child, sooner. We also were open to twins or even a sibling group if the sibling was under three years of age. I was afraid to adopt an older child for fear of trauma, which could lead to psychological issues.

With our research complete and our country chosen, the next step was to pull together a big stack of official documents called a dossier. I was determined to get everything organized as quickly as possible to speed up the process. The dossier took time and coordination to get everything completed. We had to get our fingerprinting done both locally and through Homeland Security. There were medical exams for a clean bill of health and scheduling notaries for these exams as well. The INS forms needed completion, which in our case was the Form I-600 A since Vietnam was a non-Hague Convention country participant. We needed letters from employers, referral letters from friends, and lots of notarizations of all documents. Fueled by excitement and determination, I managed to pull together the entire dossier in just under three months—an achievement my agent called record-breaking for their agency. I was truly delighted at what I had accomplished, and every checklist I completed brought me one step closer to the family I'd been dreaming of.

About six weeks later, I received a letter from the U.S. Department of Homeland Security that stated they were unable to complete the processing of our application—a red flag had appeared. It turned out there was an old arrest on my record. I had thought the arrest had happened when I was 17 and that the charges had been expunged but apparently I was 18 at the time. Even though the charges were dropped, it still showed up. I guess my memory had conveniently expunged my actual age from my brain!

Suddenly, I felt totally exposed and judged, frustrated that something from so long ago was making this process even more difficult—especially when all I wanted was to build a loving family.

Now I had just 45 days to prove what happened with that old arrest—which meant submitting official court records to finish our adoption application for Vietnam. The panic set in as I scrambled to track down decades' old paperwork. I emailed the Portland police, only to be told I had to ask the county court instead. When I called them, there was no record at all—it had been more than 20 years! Desperate, I asked my sister Bonnie, who lived close by, to search their archives in person, but even she turned up empty-handed. It all felt surreal and frustrating—like my entire future was being put on hold by a dark shadow from my past that had disappeared without a trace.

Frustrated and running out of options, I emailed the Portland Police Bureau yet again—this time to explain what the Multnomah County Court had told me. I also explained how the charges had been dropped, and it never went to court. The arresting officer never showed up, and the Portland Police Bureau had no documentation either. The whole thing was turning into a maddening loop, and I couldn't believe how complicated it had become just to get one simple answer. The only record was that of a case number. The arrest record was all that showed up. I asked what they suggested I do at this point. The response was more promising. A police department coworker had suggested to request a certified copy of a Criminal History Check. They said this should note the status of the case, and I was given a website to access this request. A glimmer of hope lit up in my heart.

With a bit of relief, I went to the website and wrote a detailed letter explaining my request, outlining everything I had done to try to obtain my old record. Eventually, I was told that the charge of hindering prosecution had been dropped— the citing officer never showed up to court, and no further action was taken. I then received official confirmation that no record was found, so I wrote a letter to Homeland Security explaining the situation. It was a welcome respite when I learned that was enough to satisfy them.

Being scrutinized is something we may have to endure in our lives, and it was a very uncomfortable feeling. The whole situation started with an incredibly uncomfortable misunderstanding. I had simply dropped off a friend, not knowing they had a warrant out for their arrest. I wasn't even pulled over while my friend was in the car—it happened afterward, once they were already gone. Apparently, officers had tried to wave me down, but I hadn't noticed. Later, they claimed that I had somehow "abetted" my friend in avoiding arrest, but I had no idea what was going on. It felt so unfair to be caught up in something I hadn't understood at all, and the entire experience left me feeling anxious and shaken. I wished I hadn't had to relive that moment, but it was all cleared up, and we were on to the next phase of our adoption.

Next came the home study, where a social worker visits your home and conducts interviews over a period of time. The interviews were somewhat invasive, covering questions about previous abuse, mental health, drug and alcohol habits or addiction, legal issues, full financial analysis and disclosure, education, religious beliefs, and childhood family life and trauma. We were interviewed separately and together. Parenting classes were also needed. The scrutiny of the home study felt like living under a microscope. Every part of my life—my habits, relationships, beliefs, even my home—was examined and questioned. It was hard not to feel exposed and judged, constantly wondering if I measured up while every detail was dissected.

In this part of the adoption process, we were required to attend several hours of classes about the importance of keeping a child's culture alive, bonding, and what to expect in terms of an international adoption. This included questions that might arise, possible scenarios we could face, or challenges we might encounter along the way. These classes would continue after the adoption as well.

And then there was the waiting time.

The waiting time is the period in which we are waiting for our referral, when we are matched with our child. We were told that Vietnam looks at the dossier and uses numerology to help them match the adoptee with the adoptive parents. This can be what takes the longest. The waiting was incredibly difficult—it felt like time was moving at a glacial pace, each week stretching endlessly into the next. In our case, it took so long that we had to update many parts of our dossier, which expired after a year. We had to redo medical exams and fingerprints and notarize paperwork all over again. It was arduous and exhausting to repeat all the steps we'd already completed, all while anxiously waiting for any signs of progress.

Then, in April of 2008, everything changed when we were told that there were some discrepancies in the adoption process for Vietnam—and that the U.S.A. was investigating corruption. There was speculation that Vietnam would possibly be closing adoptions if they didn't comply with the demands of the U.S.A. A few weeks later, Vietnam halted accepting any new dossiers for adoptions to the U.S.A. This was quite a blow. Here I was at an impasse. The U.S. government was accusing Vietnam of corruption in its adoption process—baby trafficking and bribery to poor birth moms. Was I about to lose another child? Were these accusations true? Did they have any real merit? I started to panic.

A few weeks later, the disagreement between countries resulted in Vietnam not accepting any new dossiers for adoptions to the U.S.A. The agreement between countries would expire in September. If an agreement were not reached, then anyone who had not received a referral by September 1st would not be allowed to continue their adoption. That meant if I didn't get a referral, I would have to start over in a different country. A year and a half of our time and energy invested, and so much money wasted. More importantly, I would be losing another child. Would I even want to start over? What if I did start over, and everything fell apart again? The thought of four more months of excruciating, uncertain waiting was almost unbearable.

Waves of anxiety began to wash over me, and eventually depression hit me as the long, uncertain journey wore me down. The constant waiting left me feeling exhausted and hopeless, and I started to doubt whether I could keep going at all. Desperate for support, I reached out to a counselor, looking for someone to help me carry the pain. During one agonizing appointment, I broke down and confessed that I didn't want to live anymore. The intensity of what I shared with my therapist caused her to insist that I not be left alone, suggesting I be put on a 72-hour hold for my safety. I panicked at the idea—suddenly terrified by the prospect of being hospitalized and losing what little sense of control I still had. Although my husband was out of town on a business trip, I convinced my therapist to talk to him on the phone. He assured her I would be safe if I stayed with a friend after talking me down. So, I called a close friend for help. She picked me up and together we agreed—both formally and out of true concern—that she would stay by my side and keep me safe until the darkness began to lift. I felt exposed and vulnerable, but deeply grateful not to be alone.

After that experience and everything I had been through, I realized I needed more support to make it through the waiting. So that summer, while still waiting for a referral, I enrolled in two group therapy programs—one focused on depression and another on anxiety. It was a step I took for myself, determined to find some healing and strength as I continued the long journey.

This turned out to be a remarkably healing experience. It was reassuring to know I wasn't alone in my pain. Sharing my story and listening to other people's stories offered me comfort. It helped ease some of the loneliness and fear I'd been carrying, and brought a small but vital sense of peace back into my life. I had quite the support group rooting for me. Hearing others' problems and how they were handling them made me realize I was not doing so poorly after all. I was much stronger than I had thought.

Another well-needed distraction also presented itself that summer—my nephew came to stay with us. He and his parents were having a difficult time navigating ADHD and the teen years. I offered to take him in and structure his summer with learning and activities. As a teacher I had the summer off, so this was a win-win for all. Having him around brought a deep sense of comfort; caring for him allowed me to embrace the mothering side of myself that I had been yearning to express. We had a regular schedule for learning, tutoring, and fun social activities. He would practice his violin every day and work on projects. His presence filled the house with laughter and light, and tending to his needs gave me a renewed sense of purpose. It distracted me from the endless anxiety of waiting and helped keep the darkest feelings of depression at bay.

I enjoyed creating summer fun for him. I set up a teen hangout at the waterpark. We went to the Bay Area, where he got to hang out with his grand uncle. We drove to Ashland to visit his grandfather. While there, we went rafting on the Rogue River. His laughter and joy continued to fill my heart. We even drove up to Portland to visit his cousins, aunt, and uncle. His uncle, Jeff, took him fishing, and he caught a sturgeon over three feet in length. For a while, instead of being consumed by uncertainty, I could pour my love and attention into someone who needed me right then and there. I loved sharing all these new experiences with him. It was the perfect summer distraction.

The summer's end was quickly approaching, and I still had not received a referral. Each day, I had to draw upon my courage to check my email—bracing myself for yet another day of no news, but still clinging to hope for the answer that could make my dream come true. It was now August 29th and still no word. The September 1st deadline was getting too close for comfort. My nephew would be leaving soon, and I would be going back to work.

That afternoon I went into my office and opened my email. There was an email from the adoption team. I was so nervous, not knowing if it was going to be good or bad news. My pulse raced as my eyes darted over the first few words. The first word was "Congratulations!" My breath caught, and I read it again, barely able to believe what I was seeing. For so long, this had felt impossible—now suddenly, it was real. And then two pictures of the most amazing little boy I had ever seen. I yelled to my nephew, "Hurry, David! Come in here!" I couldn't believe it. I was finally a mom!

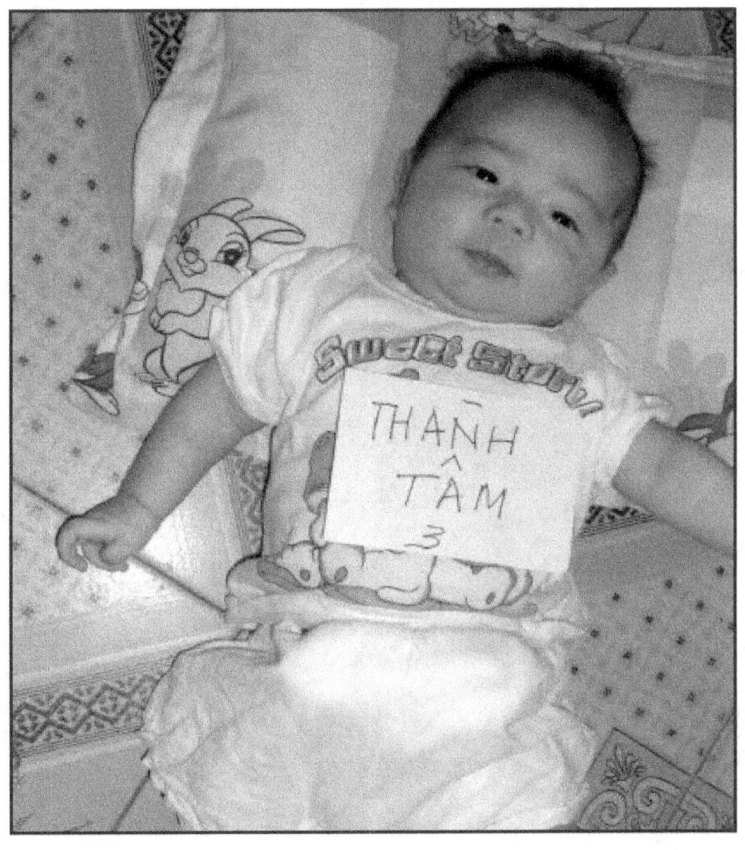

Section 4

From Waiting to Welcome: Our Family Begins

With our adoption nearly complete, we prepared for our journey to Vietnam, hearts full of anticipation. After so much waiting, we were finally on our way to meet our child and take the first steps into life as a family.

Chapter 10

Our son's name was Thanh Tam and he had been born on April 23, 2008, in Da Nang, Vietnam. He was four months old and absolutely perfect. We were going to raise a son. Words couldn't express the joy that I felt, the years of hoping and dreaming finally becoming a reality. My heart was so full. This had been a long time in the making.

We continued to receive information about our son while waiting to hear about our travel date. We discovered that he had been left at the gate of Da Nang Orphan Fostering Center. Through translation, we received this letter from the staff member who found him:

"Now I make this application to present for discovering THANH TAM, abandoned child dated on April 23, 2008, as follows:

At 22h30 as the same date, I bought something for dinner; discovering abandoned child at gate of Center. Immediately I embraced a child into center after that I announce Ms. Hue, Head of 3D Woman Association to wit. Through checking, a child weights 3.2 kg, health status was normal. The child wore a heart-pink pull, with an orange nappy; he was covered with light yellow shaped large towel. He had lost umbilical cord. Then Center announces the Ward Registrar to make the minutes 8h00' on April 24, 2008. I undertake the above information is true and exact; I will take full responsibility if mistaking."

There had been a public announcement via various public media—radio and newspaper—about the abandoned child for over a month. We even received a newspaper with the announcement. Once the time allocated for local families to come forward had passed, and no one stepped forward to adopt Thanh Tam, the director of the center made the decision to allow him to be matched with a family outside of Vietnam. We received the wonderful news on August 29, 2008.

We were overjoyed each time we received updated photos of our precious son. Although he was growing without our hands to hold him, it meant the world to us to see how he was changing and thriving, even from afar. Each new picture brought us so much happiness, allowing us to witness his growth and development despite the distance. The medical exams we received reassured us that he was healthy and well cared for, which brought us comfort as we waited to finally be with him.

We obtained many official documents that comforted us in the legitimacy of the adoption. Given the earlier allegations of bribery and trafficking, I felt a great deal of anxiety. I would have been devastated if our child had been taken from his birth parents. The information that was sent out from the Vietnam government was adamant that this was unlikely and that the intra country adoption was monitored very closely. But still, there was that thought that had been put into the back of my mind; the "what if" mantra that this intrusion creates.

As I waited to meet our son, I searched for ways to soothe my fears and find some peace of mind. I found comfort in visiting a family who had just returned from Vietnam and was able to meet their son. I joined a support group that met monthly for dinner to discuss their recent adoptions and others who were in the waiting period. I felt blessed that we had not chosen Russia or Ukraine. The stories were frightening.

I received a letter from a family we met at a meeting regarding the Ministry of Labor, Invalids, and Social Affairs in Vietnam—a government agency that oversees and regulates the adoption process within Vietnam. They had recently returned from Vietnam with their baby:

Hi Barbara,

I don't know if you remember me, but we sat next to each other at one of the *MNO meetings and you were, understandably, going through a really hard time because you and your husband hadn't received your referral yet from Vietnam. We went to the Heartsent picnic today and Steven told me you FINALLY received it on 8/29/2008. CONGRATULATIONS!!!!!!!!!!!

I have asked, along our journey, each and every time we met with Steven whether you had received your referral yet. Believe it or not, each time, I had such empathy for you guys to hear you hadn't. Who the hell knows what order there is to any of this? Oh! I know - there is none.

Since you have to be feeling a bit better now, I wanted to contact you and say, besides hello, that we returned on Aug. 8th from Vietnam with our precious daughter. I could go on and on about the experience of being in Vietnam (which was amazing), but that's not what I'm writing about.

This is about you and yours—and what I hope will not be a long time before you receive word to travel. The doctor and her staff are top-notch, and you will be well taken care of. And hopefully you will experience much LESS tropical humidity than we did. Is your son in northern or southern VN? My daughter was in Hanoi. So we were fortunate to not have to make two travels.

Anyway, there are few of us from Vietnam, so it would be great to stay in touch and if I can help you with any travel tips, let me know. My daughter is amazing and so is your son. I am so happy for you and the biggest part of the waiting is hopefully a thing of the past!

Take care.

XXXX

We were deeply grateful for all the support we received during this waiting period. Each encouragement and bit of help brought us one step closer to completing our journey. Then, on November 19, 2008, we received a letter from the U.S. Citizenship and Immigration Services (USCIS) notifying us that they had received our Petition to Classify Orphan as an Immediate Relative(Form I-600) We were thrilled to learn that USCIS had determined that the child identified as Tam Thanh qualified as an orphan, as defined by section 101 (b)(1)(F) of the Immigration and Nationality Act, as amended.

This sounded so official, although it wouldn't be until the adoption was completed in Vietnam and final papers were presented for our baby's visa. One step closer. The anticipation was killing me—I was buzzing with excitement, but also filled with nerves, knowing that soon I would finally be there, meeting my son at last. Every day felt longer as we waited, my heart racing, knowing I'd soon be holding our child for the first time.

To celebrate, my good friend offered to throw a baby shower for me. What made it really memorable was that men were also invited—it was actually my first coed baby shower, and it had such a fun, lively energy. One of the highlights (or maybe lowlights!) was the hilarious game where you open a diaper and have a guess what kind of smashed candy bar is inside. It was honestly pretty gross, but the men absolutely loved it and were cracking up the whole time. The day was full of laughter and support from everyone around us, and it truly made everything feel more real and exciting as we prepared to welcome our child.

A little later, the excitement followed me right into my classroom when my homeroom mom threw me a baby shower with my class. That year, I was teaching first grade, and their celebration was truly one of the sweetest—and most entertaining—surprises. She had each of the kids make me a colorful handprint cutout with advice for a new mom written on them and strung them together to be hung on the wall. I proudly hung their masterpiece in the baby's room, and every time I read their words, I burst out laughing—so much honesty, so many gems, and only the kind of advice a first grader could think up. Those joyful, funny messages became a real treasure during the home stretch of our adoption journey. A reminder that we were loved and cheered on by this bunch of adorable goofballs.

Chapter 11

I will never forget the moment—December, the crisp air—when the call finally came. "Get ready to travel." My heart simply exploded. All the anticipation, all the late night what ifs, and crossed fingers were finally answered. This was the moment we counted down to, the one I had dreamed of for so long. I was equal parts thrilled and terrified. It was real—we were finally traveling to Vietnam to get our son.

Thankfully, my job as a teacher meant I would have two weeks off during Christmas break —which felt like a small miracle in the middle of this whirlwind. The timing couldn't have been better, but things got tricky: my maternity leave would be only six weeks if I gave birth to a baby, but as an adoptive mother, my "leave" was technically only two days. Apparently, maternity leave was really just medical leave, and adoption didn't count. So, while we would be gone from December 23 to January 9, I would have to use three of my precious personal days to cover the overlap. Even that couldn't dim my happiness. I was about to become a mother, and no hurdle would stop me.

Christmas had never felt this magical. We booked our flight with China Airlines to leave December 24 at 12:15 a.m. from San Francisco to Ho Chi Minh City (Saigon) with a layover in Taipei, Taiwan. The stars had truly aligned for us—arriving at 10:05 a.m. on Christmas day felt like unwrapping the best present of my life.

At the airport, we were greeted by our in country adoption guide, Madame Nguyen. Warm, welcoming, and fluent in English, she immediately put us at ease. Her expertise was apparent as she brought us to our hotel and laid out our itinerary for the days to come. Everything felt amazingly exciting and dreamlike—I could hardly believe we had finally arrived. We checked into the Lan Lan 2 Hotel in District 1, right in the heart of the city, with so many tourist attractions within walking distance. There was a thrill in the air, mixed with a quiet happiness and gratitude, as if everything we'd hoped for had somehow come together on this special Christmas morning.

We were to meet with two separate single female adoptive parents. One of the women was a Caucasian American lawyer from Colorado who had traveled with her sister. She had previously adopted three children from China and wished to adopt another, but China had too long of a wait, so she chose to adopt a boy from Vietnam. The other woman was African American from Southern California and had previously adopted children in America. She was adopting a baby girl. We would spend much of our time traveling and conducting adoption business together. Having them by our side during such an overwhelming and emotional process brought us immense comfort. Simply knowing we weren't alone—having people nearby who understood our worries, hopes, and daily challenges—made everything feel less daunting. We quickly built a sense of camaraderie, offering each other a shoulder to lean on and celebrating every milestone, big and small. Their companionship brought warmth and comfort to our days, and their empathy was a constant source of reassurance whenever we needed it. In this unfamiliar country, facing so many uncertainties, their presence felt like a circle of support, turning strangers into friends and transforming our journey into something more manageable and uplifting. I can only hope we were able to offer them the same comfort and encouragement that we so gratefully received.

We had time in between business to be tourists and delve into the culture of Vietnam. Staying in District 1 made it easy to walk to all the tourist attractions. We shopped at the Ben Thanh Market, which is an enormous open-air marketplace with local food, clothing, handicrafts, textiles, art, souvenirs, and an abundance of haggling. It wasn't uncommon to get fantastic bargains and excellent deals at the market. This was such a lively place and an amazing first experience for us to dive right into the lifestyle of the locals. Beyond the hustle and bustle of the market, we also shopped for baby clothes at Saigon Centre, which is a beautiful, enclosed mall with high-end stores and luxury items.

The streets were abuzz with motorbikes and a disarray of traffic with nary a traffic light in much of the city. Pedestrians would cross at their own risk. We became aware that seatbelts and helmets were not required, kids riding on the front and backs of scooters, with exhaust creating so much pollution. Many of the motorbike drivers and riders wore masks to ward off the health effects of the carbon monoxide.

We spent a day walking through Tao Dan Park, visiting the Mariamman Hindu Temple, The Reunification Palace, Saigon Notre Dame Basilica, and several street vendors and boutiques. We were definitely getting the flavor of the city.

Christmas decor was all around. This was a most magical Christmas for sure.

We had a flight scheduled for Da Nang on the 28th to meet our son and officiate the adoption. We decided to spend the night before our flight preparing ourselves for the most exciting engagement of our lives. The spas in Vietnam were ridiculously inexpensive, so we booked a day at one. It was so lovely and relaxing. The nerves began to settle, jet lag dissipated, and we ended our night with a nourishing, wholesome meal. We were ready to do this!

The next morning, all three families flew from Ho Chi Minh City to Da Nang on December 28. Da Nang is a beautiful coastal city in central Vietnam. We were escorted by van to the Da Nang Orphan Fostering Center where we all were to meet our babies. The van was brimming with anticipation. Being our first adoption, and after seventeen years of longing—years marked by hopes rising and falling like the tide—we found ourselves absolutely buzzing with excitement. Our hearts tender with gratitude for the promise to come. For us, this was a chapter written after so many patient seasons—a dream finally beginning to take shape before our eyes.

We arrived at the orphanage, my eyes tracing over the rows of cribs—so many tiny lives nestled together, three or four to a bed. I then scanned the room for my son, and then my heart surged as I saw his sweet face. When Thanh Tam was placed in my arms, a feeling of warmth and jubilation surged through my body. I was so enamored with this sweet child. I had never felt so much love. It was then that I realized that loving this child was not going to be difficult in the slightest. This moment felt so right.

We took several pictures, wanting to soak up every precious second with him, our hearts overflowing with joy. But along with the excitement, it was bittersweet to know we'd have to leave our son at the center for another night before we could take him into our care in the morning. So, we made the most of the time we had, quietly wishing we didn't have to say goodbye, even for just one more night.

After our goodbyes, we went to the Royal Hotel where we would spend two nights. One without our son and another, our first night with our son. The excitement of knowing we would be adopting Thanh Tam the next day was augmented by the celebration in the streets that night. Just up north at the My Dinh National Stadium in Hanoi, Vietnam had just won the final in the men's ASEAN Football Federation (AFF) Championship (officially known as the AFF Suzuki Cup) against their all-time rival, Thailand. The excitement and patriotism of the raucous crowd spread throughout Vietnam. The streets of Da Nang were on fire with enthusiasm. We felt that this was a good omen and celebration of our long and arduous journey into parenthood. Tears flowed from my eyes.

The next day was a glorious morning, and we were on our way to pick up our babies and travel to the Peoples Committee to legalize our adoption on December 29th. All three families sat around a large rectangular table with several people from the Peoples Committee. My husband was the person with whom most of the communication was directed. We assumed because he was the only male. It was a lengthy and somewhat intimidating meeting. All of us very independent and strong women kept quiet for fear that something might go awry if we said anything perceived as "out of line." Once the meeting was concluded, the paper-work was completed, and we were now allowed to officially take custody of our adopted babies. Our now 8-month-old son was ours! This was the most surreal moment I had ever encountered. Taking official custody of our son filled me with an incredible sense of relief and pure joy. Although we still had a journey ahead—immunizations, paperwork, and travel documents—finally holding him in our arms as his parents made all the waiting worthwhile. The overwhelming mix of gratitude and happiness in that moment is something I will never forget. Now it was time to bond.

Back at the hotel, we were filled with awe and gratitude for what we had accomplished together. After so many years of hoping, waiting, and longing for this moment, we had finally reached our dream of parenthood. We held him close, fed him, played, and laughed with him—then watched as he drifted into a sound sleep. Every tiny cry and whimper felt like a miracle to us; he was beautiful in every way, and our hearts flowed with love just to be near him. We had a most precious son. The universe had come through. The real journey had just begun. We named him James, a family name on both sides of the family, and Preston because we liked how it sounded with James. We also gave him a middle name of Binh, which is Vietnamese for peace. James Preston Binh, our baby boy, *our* baby boy.

The next morning, we flew back to Ho Chi Minh City to complete the medical exam and get vaccinations. We would remain there for five more days. We checked back in to the same hotel as we had previously stayed, but there was no crib for our little guy. So, I lined my suitcase with soft blankets and made a tiny bed for him. Seeing him curled up and sleeping soundly in that improvised cradle was the sweetest sight—he looked absolutely adorable, and I couldn't help but smile at our creative solution and the simple joy of having him so close.

James was so sweet, and it warmed my heart to see how much he seemed to enjoy our attention and being held. I noticed that the back of his head was a little flat, which made me wonder about the time he'd spent lying on his back. With only a couple of caregivers for thirteen babies, and just four cribs between them, I imagined the nursery had been a little crowded. At eight months he still couldn't roll over, and he had quite a rash on his face and body. There were also a few darker spots on his skin, which at first looked like bruises to me. But I remembered we'd been told ahead of time that these were completely normal—what they called Mongolian spots—and that they were common in Asian babies and would fade with time. I also noticed that he would get overheated easily and start to sweat, so I was grateful our hotel room had air conditioning.

Already, I found myself watching him closely, learning to notice all the little things—his comfort, his needs, the tiniest changes. It made me realize how sweet it felt to care for him in this new way, how much love and attention I wanted to give to our precious boy. More than anything, I just felt so lucky and excited to finally have this time with him, to care for him, and start getting to know our sweet son.

We had a couple days to play before the vaccinations, so in the meantime we took our son sightseeing. We went to the Saigon Zoo and Botanical Garden. It was a beautiful sunny day and most of the animals were out and full of entertaining antics for our sweet baby boy. The monkeys were playful, and the hippos were basking in the sun. The river otters were sliding through the water slides. The best part, though, was when we visited the elephants. They were close enough to pet and feed, so we bought some food and James got to feed them. His sweet chocolate brown eyes lit up with joy and amazement. It is no wonder that this sizable creature with its impressive trunk became his favorite animal. Of course, we recorded this moment and years later, rewatched it with James. The excitement in his eyes returned when he heard his own delightful baby laughter.

We also took a short tour of the History Museum of Ho Chi Minh City and the Ton Duc Thang Museum before getting dinner and enjoying the New Year festivities in the park. It was not the Lunar New Year celebration—unfortunately we would miss that by a couple of weeks—but New Year's was still a big celebration with festive fireworks. James really enjoyed seeing that.

The next day we went to some museums, including the War Remnants Museum, which had graphic depictions of the "American War" as it is called there. I was a child during the war and only recall the scenes that were shown on the news, and the five young refugee men that our church sponsored after the war ended. This museum gave us a completely different perspective of the war and a deeper understanding of what my husband's father had experienced as a veteran of this ravishing and devastating war. Still to this day, you can see the effects of Agent Orange on the forthcoming generations. Deformities, crippled by being born with missing limbs...

That evening we went to watch a live show at the Golden Dragon Water Puppet Theatre. I know he doesn't remember, but James was quite aware at the time, and his smile showcased his amusement. I must admit I also found the show quite entertaining. We wanted to give him as much exposure to his culture before we returned to America.

The next morning was vaccination day. Before we left, James rolled over for the very first time. His first milestone with us—and I was absolutely tickled to witness it, grinning with pride at this tiny but amazing achievement. I guess having the extra space and all the attention got him moving—it's amazing what a little room to wiggle and a cheering section can do. All three families had breakfast together at the hotel and then took a van to the medical clinic.

Our adoption guide helped us to get the paperwork completed and got us situated at the clinic. Honestly, I was a bit anxious to be at this place. I had read several articles recently about side effects of vaccinations and was a bit horrified by what had changed since I was a child receiving vaccines. However, people did it regularly and it was a requirement in the adoption process, so I tried not to worry and take what I had learned with a grain of salt.

When it was time to go into the room with the doctor for our son's vaccinations, we all marched over with our babies. But as soon as we arrived, things took an unexpected turn. Our son was taken while all the other parents and their babies were ushered in together. We were pushed aside—not knowing the language, it was all so confusing. I felt a tinge of panic pulse through my body but didn't want to cause a commotion. After all, we were so close to finally getting our child and returning home with him, that I didn't want anything to go wrong at this point. We were in a communist country where adoptions were now closed to the United States and women had fewer rights than men. I had to control my motherly instinct to want to protect my child. So, we waited, for what felt like an eternity.

Finally, the door opened and everyone, including James, came out. He was crying and I took him into my arms to comfort him—and probably myself as well. The other moms assured me that all went well although James had been crying throughout. I felt so overcome with guilt for not being there with him. We all left and went back to the hotel to rest.

Within hours I noticed a distant look in James' eyes and then he began to have some problems breathing. I was not sure what was happening, but I immediately started to wonder what had happened in that room during the medical exam and vaccinations. Did something happen that the other moms didn't catch because of the language barrier? Paranoia began to seep into my mind. I continued to monitor him and prepare for tomorrow's flight to Hanoi for his visa. His breathing continued to be a bit labored, but at least it didn't seem to get any worse.

Our last breakfast in Ho Chi Minh on Jan 3, 2009, was followed by checking out and traveling to Hanoi. We all piled into the van and headed to the airport, full of anticipation for this next and final leg of our adoption journey. The flight itself was only two hours. The kids, already seasoned travelers, handled the flight wonderfully. When we landed in Hanoi, we were taken straight to our hotel, the Cherry Hotel 2. Hanoi was smaller than Ho Chi Minh, but still a bustling and vibrant city. We were happy to discover some vegetarian restaurants, but our favorite quickly became the Tamarind Cafe, which we visited several times due to the delicious and fresh vegetarian food. It felt amazing to be so close to bringing our child home, and the excitement kept building with each new step.

We had been told to expect strangers to want to hold our baby while in Vietnam, and this place was no exception. The staff at the Tamarind Cafe were incredibly friendly—they lit up when we arrived and whisked James off to the kitchen, adoringly showing him off to the kitchen crew. This was repeated each time we came back. Definitely different than the U.SA.

While awaiting our appointment for James' visa, we spent much of our time walking or taxiing around the city, enjoying the shopping and the parks mostly. The Vietnam National Arts Museum was huge and took several hours to visit. This place had amazingly beautiful artwork and artifacts. It was gorgeously displayed and spanned several centuries. We wanted to soak in as much of the culture and take lots of pictures for James to enjoy and learn about as he got older.

There was a lovely garden with a lotus and lily pad pond. Although the lotuses weren't in bloom in January, a few of the lily flowers had begun to blossom.

There were many aesthetically pleasing landscapes and architecture. Saigon had its share of French architecture and influence, but it seemed like Hanoi had more. There were some great open air and street markets and women walking around with giant baskets on their heads. Many women were also seen walking with two baskets balanced on a pole over their shoulder (shoulder pannier baskets) wearing conical hats (nan la). One woman took off her hat and put it on my head and tried to get me to carry her baskets. Definitely talented women.

On one particular day, a woman said to me how cute my baby was and that he had a good nose. James loved the constant attention from the locals. Another stopped me to say how much he looked like me. Good to know that a sense of humor seemed to be a common trait in Vietnamese culture. I hoped this would be a trait in James.

Bathroom experiences in Vietnam were often squat toilets and lacked toilet paper. We were told to be prepared for this. Trying to hold a baby and squatting was no easy task, and I appreciated having my husband there to hold James. Nowadays there seem to be more Western style toilets, but in 2008-09, most of the public toilets we used were on the ground squatters.

All this time with James was such fun, sharing his culture, mingling with the locals, but my favorite was just hanging out in the hotel and trying on cute boy outfits and playing with his cool new toys. Just the simple things were the best. On January 7th we visited the U.S. Embassy and Consulate in Vietnam, Hanoi for the Intercountry Adoption Visa. Before the visit we had to obtain the final I-600 approval and submit the following:

- Vietnamese Passport for the beneficiary
- 4 passport-size photos for the beneficiary
- $400 application fee, payable in USD cash or credit card
- Completed immigrant visa application form DS-230
- Medical forms: DS-2053, DS-3024, DS-3026
- Vaccination Affidavit DS-1981

We had such a great team helping us navigate through everything, giving us time to go back to our hotel for a nap—a much-needed respite. During the immigrant visa interview, the consular officer reviewed the I-600 petition and immigrant visa application, looked over our child's medical condition and examination report, and confirmed the required travel documentation. If everything was in order, we could return the following day for the visa. One step closer, and the anticipation continued.

The next day we went back to the U.S. Embassy and thankfully discovered that everything was in order to obtain the visa. James received the visa to travel to the United States, where upon arrival, he would become a citizen of the United States of America. He would be allowed to return at 18 to get his dual citizenship if he wished. So, we went back to our hotel to prepare for our return home as a family. It was another bitter-sweet moment. The other two families were a day ahead of us and had already left on their flight to America. Though we were excited to get home and show James his new bedroom and meet his new relatives, we had really loved our time in Vietnam, immersing ourselves in our son's culture.

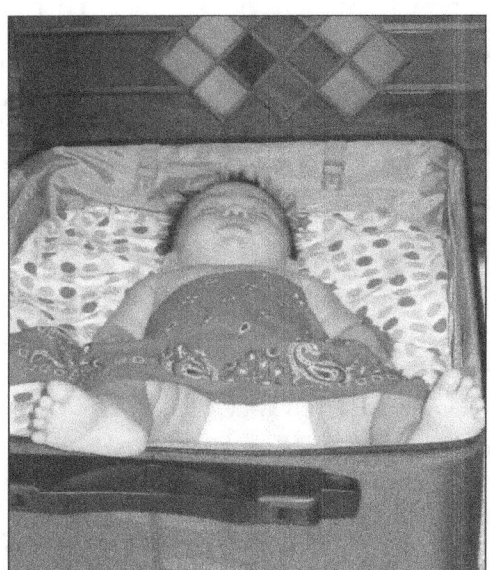 

Chapter 12

After years and years of hope, heartache, and determination, culminating in a journey halfway across the world, the moment finally arrived—we were going home as a family. Home. A word that now meant so much more than it ever had before we left the country to bring our son back with us. After all we had been through, "home" was no longer just a place; it became a feeling, a promise, and a newfound sense of belonging. We were on our way home. We were, at last, a family.

January 9, 2009, we flew from Hanoi to Taiwan for a layover, where we were greeted by a delightful surprise—the airport was filled with painted cows, decorated in vibrant colors and playful patterns. James was enchanted, pointing excitedly at each one and laughing with pure joy. Watching him marvel at these whimsical works of art made the layover feel magical, turning an ordinary airport stop into a memory we'll always treasure. Then on to San Francisco where my Uncle Bill and friend, Connie, were waiting at the baggage claim to welcome us home. Connie gave James a U.S.A. beanie baby with an American flag printed across its chest. She was so excited to meet us after our long journey—having had her own struggles yet ultimately achieving success through IVF. Connie understood the importance of this moment, as she too had welcomed a beautiful son into her life. My uncle gave me a bouquet of flowers. He was especially thrilled for us as we brought our child home from Asia, having met and fallen in love with his own wife while stationed in Japan. Though they never had children of their own, he saw a reflection of his own journey in ours, and shared in our joy with a deep, personal understanding. I think he felt as though there was some vicarious living going through his heart. After we visited for a bit, we all hugged, and Connie drove us back to Sacramento.

With my school district only offering two official days of adoption leave, which I had already used, I was not discouraged. My coworkers often said I was an out-of-the-box thinker, so I made a plan for medical leave. For years I had worn high heels in which to teach and had developed a lovely bunion. It was quite convenient to schedule my surgery for when I got home with James. This would give me two weeks to adjust to being home with a new baby and still get paid leave. While I had to hop around the house during my recovery, I embraced the challenge and made the most of that precious time together. Unlike my husband, who had received paid family leave, that option was not available to me. Still, I found a way to make it work, finding strength and creativity whenever obstacles appeared on our path.

It felt so special to finally have James home in the room I had lovingly created just for him. My three favorite colors were the inspiration for the room—blue, purple, and green. Every detail was chosen with care and heart. The walls were painted a bright azure blue, making the space feel cheerful and welcoming. I painted the door, ceilings, and trim a bright white to tie the room together and add a fresh, peaceful touch. In the corner sat an old rocking chair I had lovingly refreshed with crisp white paint, next to a white wicker table—perfect for our quiet moments together—as I read him bedtime stories and rocked him to sleep. Sheer white curtains let in the sunlight while adding a soft, gentle touch. Throughout the room there were accents of purple and green—adding personality and joy. A light wood changing table, thoughtfully passed on by a friend, held two shades of light green fabric storage bins I found for his clothes and diapers. The pillows and lamp shade were adorned with green and blue stripes that echoed the joyful colors throughout the room. A couple of purple velvet pillows were tossed in, a royal touch for our little prince. A woman I had met through the adoption support group gave us a really lovely light wood crib that my husband so graciously put together. Not an easy task. The room had light oak wood floors, and I added a shag white rug. All the little touches were my way of welcoming him home, filling his first room with comfort, happiness, and all the warmth I hoped he would feel for our new beginning together.

My surgery went well, and while I was still recovering, we spent the next few weeks loving on each other. They gave me a boot to walk in, but for long distances, I needed to use crutches. The two of us crawled around on the floor together. I was so thankful to have some time at home with James but was not looking forward to being away from him when I went back to work. During this time, we had several relatives come down from Oregon in staggered visits to meet James. My mother-in-law, her daughter and granddaughter, my father, and my sister all got to meet him in his new home. I so wished my mom could have met James. Her absence was especially felt at this important chapter in my life, but in a meaningful way, she was still part of our journey—the inheritance she left us helped make the adoption possible.

One of the gifts that I had received from my family, by request, was a month of diaper service. Such a great gift for a first-time mom who was wanting to use cloth diapers. It made it so much easier to do this and not have to clean the diapers. I enjoyed the service so much that I continued to pay for it for several months. It was so much nicer using cloth now that we were home. Disposable diapers, though convenient, are expensive and have a negative impact environmentally. My mom and my sisters had used cloth diapers. I felt compelled for these reasons to continue the trend. I did, however, use the natural disposable diapers that were free from dyes and chemicals while traveling.

Just as I was starting to feel settled into managing every-thing—from diapers to sleep routines—the reality of having to leave my baby and return to work began to set in, and a deep sadness washed over me. With my return to work approaching, I knew I would need childcare. Fortunately, before we went to Vietnam, I had arranged to have my 18-year-old niece Britney from Oregon come live with us and take care of James while we worked. Even with someone I trusted, it was difficult to imagine not being there for every moment with my baby.

Britney drove down in late January and was super excited to have a new adventure. She was such a fun addition to our family. She was really into skateboarding and would take him to the skate park for entertainment. He had several teenage fans that would play with him. By the end of April, James was walking, and Britney was teaching him how to balance on a skateboard. They would dress up in cute matching outfits and take goofy pictures. I have a few with James wearing a mustache.

While Britney lived with us, she met a young man who was also into skateboarding. Eventually they fell in love and by June decided to move in together. Thankfully, since I had the summer off, I was able to spend more time with James, and Britney had the freedom to enjoy her new relationship and independence.

Chapter 13

Being a mom of a child who didn't look like me had its quirks—some days, stepping out in public felt like stepping under a microscope, every gaze magnified as people tried to make sense of us. I'm sure just being a mom in public brings attention from strangers, yet with us being different races, it made for some interesting and sometimes unnerving banter. It was 2009, and it had become a common theme to reference Brad Pitt and Angelina Jolie as "Brangelina" in the media as a celebrity pairing. Their adoption of three kids from other countries had made headlines. People often referred to my husband and me as "Brangelina" when out and about with James. Of course, they thought this was funny—but we did not. This was not a cool trend. This was seventeen years in the making for us. Even one of my coworkers, an Asian man, made a reference to "Brangelina."

Another frequent source of irritation was having strangers ask if James was my grandson. I suppose this was possible, but insulting nonetheless—especially at 43 as a first-time mom. This happened on more than one occasion. Then there were the racist comments and looks of disapproval, and the hurtful comments like "Why did you adopt from Vietnam? There are so many children who need homes in the United States." And plenty of stares. I became immune to this by staying focused in my own little bubble and not looking at people while in public. But this sense of detachment didn't happen overnight; it was something I had to build up slowly, after too many uncomfortable moments and pointed questions that left me feeling exposed and misunderstood. I realized I didn't want the stress of society to affect me and my son. Instead, I learned to draw clear boundaries. I decided it wasn't my job to educate people about my personal choices, and I protected our peace by tuning out the noise around us.

As most moms know, even when circumstances are in the "norm"— giving birth in your twenties to a child that looks like you—strangers say the strangest and most offensive things! Mom shaming seems to be a thing for some as well. I know I had probably been guilty of this when I was younger and not experienced as a mom. Judging is so unfair. I try to leave that to God these days. What's weird though is that some of the harshest looks or comments come from older folks—people you'd think would remember what it was like to have little ones in tow (and maybe a meltdown or two in the store). But honestly, it's not just the older generation. People my own age, and even younger moms, can be quick to offer their own opinions or judgments about how things "should" be done. So yes, I am now shaming the shamers. Haha. The looks you get when your child has a meltdown in the store should be filled with compassion and empathy, but often they are looks of exasperation that seem to imply "Can't you control your kid?" Moms need to be put on a pedestal rather than a pillar of shame. Hardest job in the world, with no pay and endless critique.

In my parenting classes for international adoption, I was taught to expect that some people would approach me with strange ideas or assumptions, simply because I had adopted a child of a different race than my own. I learned early on that these kinds of comments and reactions say more about other people's perspectives than they do about my family. Thanks to those classes—and my own personality—I felt more prepared to face the curiosity, questions, and even misunderstandings that came our way. It helped me to stay grounded and reminded me that there's no single "right" way to be a mom, especially in a family shaped by adoption.

Despite the mom shaming and the many unsolicited opinions that came my way, I found reassurance and community by staying connected with our adoption agency, even after we returned from Vietnam. I continued to participate in classes and reach out to the friends and support groups I'd made with other adoptive families. Surrounding myself with people who understood what our family looked like—and what it meant to walk this path—made all the difference. These were the people who could truly relate, who never asked the awkward questions, and who celebrated the joys and challenges of international adoptive parenting alongside me. Whether through support group meetings or parenting workshops, I had built a support that helped us navigate this new life—helping our family feel seen, understood, and accepted.

To help sustain those supportive connections, our agency played a role in organizing regular gatherings designed to keep our community close and offer ongoing guidance for both parents and the kids. We had enriching events every so often, such as picnics and holiday celebrations. Playdates were also made occasionally. It was suggested that we keep in touch for support both for us as parents and also our child.

At one of the events, I got to talking about the eczema that James had (the rash I had noticed previously in Saigon). One parent who had adopted her child from Vietnam mentioned that she had changed her baby's formula from cow's milk to soy formula and later goat milk. She said Asian countries don't use a lot of cow milk products and it was common for them to have an allergy to cow's milk. I took the advice and his eczema disappeared. I continued this for the next seven or eight years, occasionally introducing the dairy back into his diet. It wasn't until he was about nine that he stopped having eczema breakouts from the cow's milk.

Just as we were figuring out how to manage James' cow milk allergy, another concern was quietly unfolding each night—ever since vaccination day, he had begun to wheeze and make odd sounds in his sleep. I had decided to wait on giving him any vaccinations. About six months had passed when he had started to wheeze even more, and then he got really warm. His temperature was rising. I put him in the bathroom with hot steam to help him breathe easier. His temperature continued to go up and got to 105°. We took off for the emergency room.

By the time we arrived, and they took his temperature—it was 106.5°. Panic washed over me as the numbers registered higher than I'd ever seen or even thought possible. We got him admitted right away, and I spent the next two days and nights in his hospital room. I barely left his side, watching for every change in his breathing, and doing everything I could to make sure he was comfortable and knew I was there for him.

He was diagnosed with croup, a word that instantly made my heart clench with worry, almost as if I could feel the roughness of his cough in my own chest. That night in the hospital, each time James struggled to breathe, it felt like my own heart stopped. The sound—raspy and sharp, reminding me of a barking seal—echoed in the quiet room and made it impossible to relax. This was so scary. I thought I was going to lose him. Sitting at his bedside, helplessly watching him fight for air, I was sure I was living a parent's worst fear. All I could do was hold his tiny hand, pray, and hope I would be able to bring him home again. When we finally got the okay to leave the hospital, I felt such a wave of relief after all those fearful hours, though I was extremely exhausted.

Once he was released, we were instructed to buy a humidifier for his bedroom and told we needed to start him on an iron supplement. The iron deficiency wasn't related to his croup; it was something the doctors discovered through testing during his hospital stay. Not long after, we received a call from the doctor advising us to stop the supplement. Another doctor familiar with Asian children said that they are typically lower in iron than Caucasian children. We were relieved to know that this was not a new problem and that our son had normal iron levels. This was when we decided to find a Vietnamese doctor for his pediatrician.

Dr. Pham became his primary doctor, and she was wonderful. Having grown up in Vietnam, moved to the U.S. as a teenager, and graduated from Dartmouth, she brought both understanding and expertise to his care. Over time we learned that his wheezing was actually asthma, and we were able to find natural ways to help curb his breathing problems.

Right after we got home from the hospital, I had a trip planned for an Alaskan Cruise. My father had invited me and my two sisters to go on a 10-day cruise. This would be the first time we all went on a vacation together. My parents had divorced when I was one, and the last time we had all gone away together was when I was five years old. I was torn over whether I should go. How could I leave my son when he had just been in the hospital? My dad had already paid for the trip, and since my dad was now 80 years old, this was possibly the last time we would have this opportunity. I was reluctant to leave my little boy after his croup episode. This was a difficult decision, both because I felt guilty—after everything it took to finally become a mom and now leaving him just six months after bringing him home—and because I was frightened that he might get sick again and I wouldn't be there to comfort him. James was now 14 months old, so the guilt and worry were only eased by the reassurance and support from my husband and niece. Britney assured me she would be available to care for James whenever Michael needed help. Even so, it was with a heavy heart and a lot of reluctance that I finally agreed to go on the cruise.

We all met in Vancouver, B.C., and stayed at a cozy bed and breakfast before boarding our ship the next afternoon. This was my first cruise, and the ship was truly luxurious, full of exciting places and new experiences. We treated my dad to a helicopter ride over a glacier—something he had always dreamed of, but never done. We went river rafting, spotted about a hundred bald eagles, and even convinced him to try zip lining and slide down a giant enclosed slide, despite his claustrophobia.

On the surface, it might have seemed like I was just on an easygoing trip. But the reality was, after loss, infertility, and a long adoption process, being away from James—even for something as memorable as this with my family—was far from easy. Guilt and worry were constant companions, and I wondered if I was being selfish having time for myself, not just as a mother. But I realized how important it is—for myself and for other parents, especially those who have fought so hard to build their families—to find time for me, outside of being a mama. As much as I loved the trip, I was eager to get home to hold James once again. Of course, he was fine and had been taken care of lovingly. Moments like this remind me it's possible to care deeply for our kids and still allow ourselves to live fully.

As summer came to an end and I prepared to return to teaching first grade, I was surprised to learn that my niece Britney and her boyfriend Sean were planning to move up to Portland, Oregon. Their news meant I would soon need to find new childcare for James, just as the school year was about to start.

After talking with my coworkers, I got the idea to ask one of my students' parents if they might be interested in helping with childcare. The thought felt like a perfect solution, and I was genuinely excited—and relieved—at the possibility. This really felt like the perfect solution: she lived close to the school, was a stay-at-home mom, and her son was the same age as James—built-in playmates for both of them. When I asked her, she said yes right away. She was happy for the extra income, and her little boy having a friend to play with. It worked out beautifully for two solid years, and I can't express the relief and gratitude I felt knowing James was so well cared for while I taught each day. As a mama, it was such a weight off my shoulders to find an arrangement that brought both comfort and joy to everyone involved.

I would pick up James right after school and bring him back to work to finish my school day. I also taught theatre and did the after-school theatre program, which James absolutely loved being a part of. He loved hanging out with the older kids and they loved having him around.

With James happily settled in with his new caregiver, I found myself able to think more seriously about the future. I had been hinting to the other first grade teacher about our hopes to adopt a baby girl. As it happened, she was moonlighting as a real estate agent, and quickly pointed out that we'd need a bigger place to make that happen. Since James wanted a little sister, and my husband and I were ready to try again, we started looking at homes together, feeling excited about this new chapter.

Six months later, we finally found a home in Cameron Park. It would be an almost hour commute to work each way, but we went from a 1,200 square foot home to a 3,300 square foot home—and a huge yard. The school district was better and the neighborhood was safer. In our current home, we had been robbed, experienced high-speed chases through our neighborhood, had shootings a couple blocks away, and our neighbor had a home invasion robbery resulting in a broken jaw and blindness in one eye. We had enjoyed living in our neighborhood otherwise; we had kind neighbors who adored James and we lived near a park that we could walk to and play. But it was time to be in a safer place at night.

Our new home needed some work, and since we decided to keep our Sacramento house as a rental, we fixed up our new house while still living in the old. Once we put in new flooring and painted, we moved in and rented out the old house. This paid for our mortgage, insurance, and taxes while leaving us with equity to collect on later. We had five bedrooms and three-and-a-half bathrooms, plus plenty of space for James to drive his firetruck and tricycle around in the house.

I decided to paint the walls in James' room the same color it had been in our Sacramento home, so the change would seem less drastic. He had a loft with a ladder and a built-in desk in his room. There was even a mirror with a ballet bar. This ended up being quite cool because after watching Peppa Pig's Ballet Lesson on television, James had asked if he could take ballet. I researched ballet classes in the area and found a ballet school in El Dorado Hills. It was a sweet school and James got lots of attention since he was the only boy. I think he enjoyed all the cute girls in their tutus.

James had developed a love for ballet and performing. I never thought I would become one of those moms who had their kids in a million extracurricular activities, but I was already looking into other activities. Never say never. You just don't know until you are in the unknown what things you will do as a parent. In fact, that summer I also enrolled him in gymnastics.

After settling into our new home, we needed to start thinking about where James would go to preschool. I researched several schools and selected a Montessori preschool near our house. My husband would drop him off in the morning after I had to leave for work, and the extended day care made it possible for me to pick him up after work. James was now three and he loved this preschool because they challenged him. One of my fondest memories was when he had been taught to recite all the presidents of the United States in order. He was so willing to perform his talent for memorizing to many willing ears.

The clock was ticking—I wasn't getting any younger, adoption came with age limits, and can take years to complete. So, now that we had settled into our new life in Cameron Park and everything was finally falling into place, we decided it was time to begin our second adoption. We got ahold of our adoption agency to start the process. We were disappointed to discover we still could not return to Vietnam. Of course, it was our first choice. Not only so James could have a sibling that looked like him, but trips back to their country of birth would be the same, thus making it easier on time and budget. Vietnam was still closed to the U.S.A.

We needed to agree on a new country. I thought back to an experience I had had about two years ago when I was driving to the gym. I was listening to Capital Public Radio and there was a story about young girls in Ethiopia who were being treated inhumanely. It was awful. Stories about female genital mutilation, child marriage, gender inequality, poverty, and health crises. But I couldn't get out of my car until the story was over. I had tears streaming down my face and wondered how I could help. I realized I could help at least one. My husband agreed and we decided on Ethiopia.

Ethiopia was the cradle of civilization and had amazing history. The people of Ethiopia were beautiful. I was so excited to be growing our family into a larger and more beautiful multicultural family. I would have to learn how to do her hair. This would be a challenge, but I was up for it.

At this point I was 46, and I knew that adoption of an infant was not going to be possible a third time with the timeline and age limits. Potentially we could again apply for the possibility of twins or a sibling set with the sibling being younger than James. After all, he was our first, and it made sense to keep his birth order. My husband wasn't quite as enthusiastic about the idea, but he agreed—with the hope we might be matched with just one baby girl this time. Of course, I secretly wished for twins since I had lost twins.

While we were getting ready to begin the adoption process again, life at work threw me a curveball. Administration decided I should switch back to Fifth Grade—a big change after finding my rhythm in First Grade. I didn't have much choice in the matter, and the timing couldn't have been worse. With limited custodial support, I found myself packing up and moving my classroom on my own. Just as the school year was beginning, I moved the wrong way and felt a sharp pain in my back. I didn't realize it then, but I had herniated a disc, and teaching was suddenly out of the question. It is not a good thing to have a sub this early in the school year, but the hernia was so painful. I ended up being out for the first four months.

At first, I had to write daily sub plans while in extreme pain, not knowing when I would return to work. After researching the internet, I was convinced that I had a herniated disc and asked my doctor for an MRI. He thought otherwise because I was not having any symptoms of sciatica, which should have accompanied a herniated disc. The MRI confirmed what I suspected—I had a herniated disc between my L4 and L5 vertebrae. I began my workers' comp benefits and physical therapy.

I was determined not to let this injury derail our plans. Even though the pain was overwhelming at times, I threw myself into physical therapy and did everything I could to heal. The thought of missing out on a chance to grow our family pushed me to work even harder—I refused to let a herniated disc keep me from being ready when the referral came. But, despite all my efforts, I still was not getting better. Eventually, I realized that surgery was the best option if I was going to be the active, present, and available parent my kids needed. The thought of having spinal surgery was so scary, but the thought of not being able to get on a plane to get my baby girl was even scarier. My doctor considered me a good candidate for a successful outcome, so I begrudgingly accepted.

The time away from work wasn't easy on me. With James at preschool, I suddenly had a lot of alone time to reflect. I found myself isolated; most of my friends were coworkers, and with no one coming to visit, loneliness started to creep in. The thought of returning to work under a principal who seemed unsupportive made me anxious. I worried about stepping back into my classroom midyear, unsure if I could reconnect with my students after they had built a routine with their substitute teacher.

During those quiet days, I would catch myself daydreaming about other possibilities, like filling out Publisher Clearing House sweepstakes and fantasizing about being a stay-at-home mom—even though realistically that wasn't something we could do financially. As the days went on, the loneliness started to weigh on me, and I could feel myself slipping into a bit of a funk.

The surgery was scheduled in late November, and I had arranged with my doctor to use December for recovery and hopefully return after Christmas break. I was so nervous to have the surgery. While the surgery went well, it left me with more time to be alone with my thoughts. Not even one of my friends or coworkers came to visit me. The only visitors in the hospital were my husband and son. Even though I was truly grateful for their support, I couldn't help but feel a little hurt that no other friends or coworkers came by. After fifteen years at this school, I began to feel uncertain about my future; teaching there no longer felt like the right path for me.

Just when I was starting to feel especially alone, an unexpected connection happened during a typical weekday activity—my son's gymnastics class. Hue, another mom, was there with her daughter and had noticed my son was wearing a shirt with Buddha on the front. Hue said they love Buddha and that they were Buddhist. After chatting for a while I discovered that they were Vietnamese. I explained that I had adopted my son in Vietnam, and we became quick friends. It was great to have met a Vietnamese family in Cameron Park. Sacramento has a fairly large Vietnamese community, but Cameron Park had very little diversity and was mostly a White community. This was no accident. I believe Divine intervention was at play because this had been a worry for me when we moved away from the city. Having a friend who grew up in Vietnam and spoke the language gave James access to his culture.

Hue was also an energy healer and had knowledge of natural products that helped reduce my back pain and helped James with his asthma. She was also an entrepreneur and got me thinking about a way out of the teaching profession.

After my back surgery, I recovered and went back to work after the Christmas/Winter break. The remainder of the year seemed longer than usual since I had to rebuild a relationship with the class—not an easy task. However, I began pursuing classes in business and dabbling in home businesses with my friend Hue. I was determined to start a new career so I could phase out of teaching and work from home to be with my kids. Although working on the adoption was foremost in my mind.

Even with so many things shifting in my professional life, our adoption journey continued to be a priority—though it wasn't without its complications. We had completed our dossier through our local agency, Heartsent. Once more, we submitted all the medical and legal requirements, including proof of employment, the last three years' tax forms, and medical insurance for the children. Again, the arrest showed up. This time I had to request two certified letters from the Portland Police Bureau with all the details. I now knew how to get this info, but I was so frustrated that I had to relive this moment again.

We continued to navigate the process, steadily submitting forms and documentation. Ethiopia required that we show our original birth certificates. My husband only had a copy, so he had to order it from Texas. I found a website that does the footwork for you and ordered through them. One more piece of our $35,000 to $40,000 adoption journey to Ethiopia.

After many weeks of preparation, we completed our home study with our Heartsent social worker. The international portion, however, required us to find a separate agency to work with. We had vetted several agencies before deciding on one. We would be adopting through International Adoption Net, IAN, located in Colorado. Once our complete dossier and home study were sent over to IAN, we continued to take classes with Heartsent while waiting to hear from IAN about the progress of our adoption.

The wait time was not as hard for me this time since I now had a child to keep me busy. Regardless, it could take longer since we had requested the sex of the child be female, and this would lessen availability in the line of other families in the world waiting for an Ethiopian baby.

I really wanted to have a girl—not just because I had a son or to balance my family, but because I was in the rare position to choose. The truth is, there was an ache in the back of my mind—a persistent worry rooted in the painful reality of raising a Black boy in this country. Stories of racial injustice, violence, and other forms of racism haunted me. I was afraid of the possibility of loss in ways I could barely admit to myself. The thought of learning to style my future daughter's hair—something that once felt daunting to me—seemed so much simpler than the fear that my son might not come home safely someday. It's a hard, uncomfortable truth to name, but it was a real part of my decision process—truth be told.

Occasionally I would call and get information about the waiting list to see where we stood in each category. I kept a journal of this. How many were ahead of us for a baby girl. Or how many were ahead of us for twins or a sibling set. The baby girl list tended to move much slower, and I would wonder if I should have been more open to a boy. But then again, we chose Ethiopia to help protect a girl from possible cruelty. What I didn't know then was our story would eventually take a wonderful, unexpected turn.

I continued to stay focused on my son and ride out the wait to bring him a sibling. Now was a time I didn't want to miss. James made this easy for me. He liked to slow me down in the wonder of the world. This, I will be forever grateful for. It is so easy to get caught up in the rat race and forget what's important. We would go on walks and jump in puddles. We looked at the flowers and the animals, and whenever I would see an airplane, we would talk about how we had flown on one to bring him home to become a forever family. We played together and read books together. He loved learning new things and I loved teaching him. It was simple, but so wonderful—these small moments of wonder and connection grounded me. Even as I waited for our family to grow, I realized with a grateful heart that I was already living the dream.

Another thing I do remember slowing down for with him was his eating style. This little man would take an hour to eat a meal. I could have followed suit and learned from him; I ate faster than anyone I knew. I was continuing to learn patience and how to slow down.

He continued his ballet and gymnastics, and we added dance and theater. He was officially very busy. In preschool he was taught the presidents of the United States in order. At the age of four, he could recite them, first and last name, and some middle names in order on command. His Montessori teacher had used hand motions to help the students do this. It was so fun to see the excitement on our friends and family's faces when he would perform this awesome feat. James was the star of Thanksgiving that year. He can no longer do this at seventeen, but he still can memorize anything he is interested in, such as all the words to the musical Hamilton.

It was around Christmas when I started thinking about the baby room. When we bought the house, the room had been painted in red and black. It was time to start painting and preparing the room. Two years had already passed since we had started the adoption process. This room was the only room we had not painted—and it was time. I chose a vivid light shade of green with bright white trim and doors. I didn't want to get too much more done since we still did not know the outcome of our referral.

One sunny, late-fall day after work—December 19th, 2012, to be exact—I was sitting outside my bank organizing my bank papers when I received a phone call from IAN. They asked if I was sitting down because they had some good news for me. I told them I was just sitting in my car about to go pick up James from school. She said they had a referral for us. My heart started speeding up, and then she said we were having twin girls. I was so excited. Tears welled up in my eyes, and I felt like the universe was a fair and gracious place. She told me to check my email for pictures. I'll never forget opening that message and seeing those faces for the first time. There they were—two of the most perfect, sweet girls, with beautiful big brown eyes and the cutest chubby cheeks. I stared in wonder, barely able to believe that I was actually going to be having twins. In that moment, the journey, the wait, and all the uncertainty fell away, replaced by a rush of excitement and joy for these precious little girls becoming my daughters. They were perfectly adorable! I immediately got off the phone and called my husband. He was ecstatic and in tears as well. I could hardly wait to tell James.

James had been so eager to meet his baby sister, but twin sisters were not what he expected. This would be the beginning of the sibling jealousy/rivalry. "I wanted one!" was the mantra from here on out, no matter what we said. The waiting for travel time had begun, and James' excitement had waned.

I had been given names of a couple other families who were traveling to Ethiopia soon so I could converse and console over waiting with them. One woman in particular, Andrea, was a big influence on me. The protocol for travel was two separate visits. On the first trip, we would travel to Ethiopia to meet the girls and appear in court to finalize the adoption. After that, we would have to leave Ethiopia without them and return home. Then about two to three months later when the visa was ready, we would return to pick up the girls. We had planned to make two quick trips and not take James, but after talking with Andrea, I started reconsidering my original itinerary. She told me that they had talked with others who had stayed in country until the visa was ready. This was apparently frowned upon by the Ethiopian adoption community. Americans were said to be aggressive and pushy when they stayed in country for the entire process. Andrea and her husband were planning to adopt their son and live in Ethiopia with him until the visa was ready. I was feeling my rebellious side awaken and this idea appealed to me as well.

After discussing it with my husband and the adoption agency, we decided we would do the same. The thought of adopting our twins and then leaving them in the orphanage for a few more months seemed so daunting. The idea of meeting them, holding them, and then having to say goodbye—knowing they would stay behind—began to feel like torture. When my friend told me about her decision to stay in Ethiopia so she could be with her child right from the start, I felt a surge of hope and relief. I loved the idea of being able to care for my daughters, to start the bond of motherhood in those very first days rather than waiting an entire ocean apart. Knowing that this could be an option felt like a choice that truly made sense to my heart. This would be our plan as well!

We were told that adopting twins would add an additional $10,000 in adoption costs. While to others that may sound like a lot, but to me, I was already completely in love with those beautiful little angels—and no price could ever compare to the joy of making them part of our family. We found a way to make it possible. We figured that if we stayed in Ethiopia we would save on airfare since we would only be traveling once. This would be great for James as well to be able to travel with us and not have to stay with someone else. The cost of living in Ethiopia was cheaper than the United States, so in the end, living there would not cost too much more than coming home and traveling back again. My father also offered to help us out a bit financially.

We planned to be there to push the process along and get back sooner. And the bonus was that we would be able to start our family with the twins much sooner. I had already lost the first few months with them. So, we went to the post office and got James a new passport.

We received this email soon after:

February 1, 2013

Hi Barbara and Michael,

The girls are doing great as you can see from the photos!!! They are just adorable.

Have a great weekend!

Aneata

Uganda and Ethiopia Program Coordinator
International Adoption Net

Each step closer was a miracle in the making. I may have wished for 14 kids as a child, but I was about to have three—which was one more than the plan when we got married. I was feeling blessed.

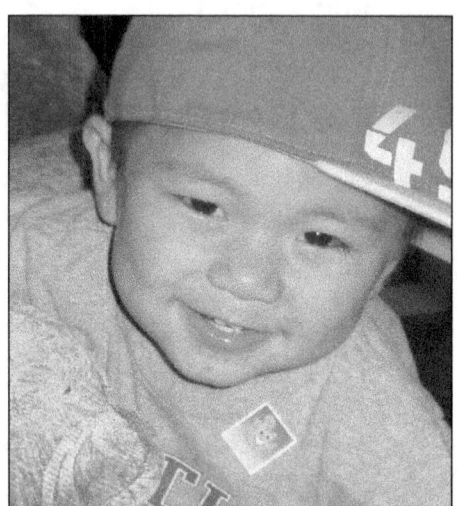

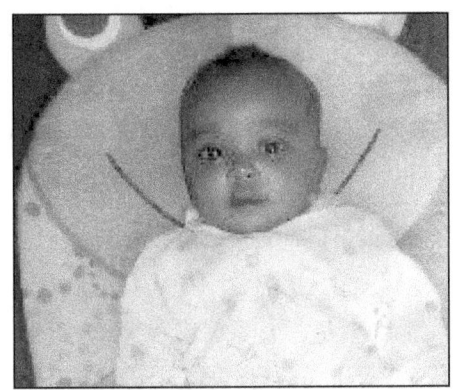
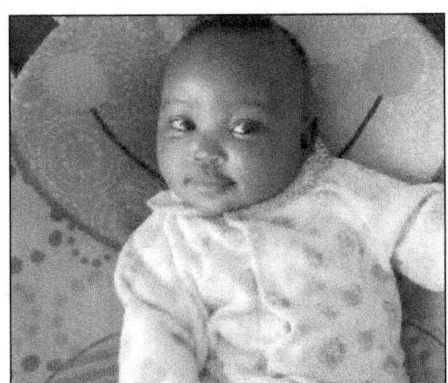

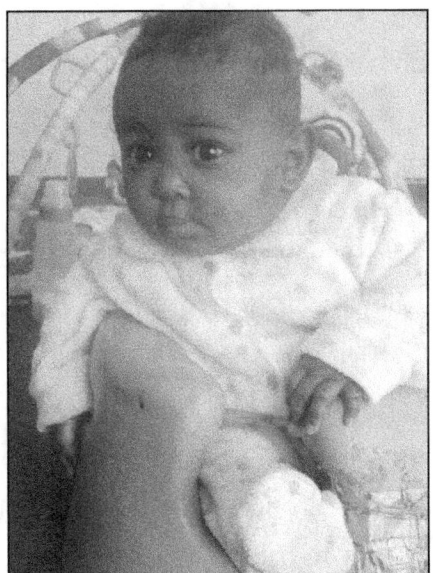

Chapter 14

They were born Marta and Merma in September of 2012. While I would soon change their names to Eliza and Zoey respectively, I could never have imagined how meeting them would forever change the very direction of my own life.

We were going to be meeting their birth mom at court during the adoption. I was nervous about meeting her. Would she be ok with her babies being raised by a White woman? Would she change her mind? And yet, I was also excited to meet her. We had no idea who Jame's birth parents were. We had more information on the girls' birth parents, but not much. All we knew about the birth parents was that their father had left, and their mother, faced with the harsh realities of poverty in Ethiopia, simply could not provide for them on her own. Out of hope for their future, she made the difficult journey from a small, tribal village in west Ethiopia to the bustling capital city of Addis Ababa, bringing her babies to the orphanage.

We had taken a class to prepare for this meeting. The first court date she was to attend was scheduled before we were to travel. However, she did not show up, and this caused a bump in our arrival time. We were told that the officials had to go to her village to look for her and bring her back to Addis Ababa. The Gambella police commission and Majag Zone police department issued public notices and asked around her village as to her whereabouts. They spent a couple months trying to locate her, but she had fled—and was nowhere to be found. There was speculation that she might have retreated to South Sudan to find work, but we never found out for sure.

Since she was not found, they rescheduled our adoption day. We would not be able to meet her after all. All we had was a picture of her holding the twins. She was young and beautiful and had lived in a small village in the Majang zone. This was all we would know. After several weeks of searching, they gave up, and our process continued without her.

The waiting time did get me thinking about what I was missing by not giving birth. I knew I would never have that experience, nor would I share those first precious months with my children—not just with my daughters, but also with James. It was sometimes difficult to listen to other moms talk about their pregnancy, birth experience, and the special bond formed through breastfeeding. I was born a woman and the one thing we women shared was the gift to bring life into this world—that gift had been taken from me. Was I truly a woman? I had heard that with hormones I could cause my body to lactate and be able to breastfeed. But were these hormones safe for me and my baby? This seemed so unnatural to me. Would my babies bond with me and would I bond with them if I was unable to breastfeed?

The looping of longing and loss played on, weaving through my adoption journey. But then, new thoughts began to cut through the loop—reminders of the small mercies and unexpected blessings. I found myself realizing how lucky I was to not endure the discomforts of pregnancy. I wouldn't have to deal with being uncomfortable as a pregnant woman in her last trimester. No sore back, swollen feet, or awkward walking. No difficulty dressing or tying shoes. I would not have to endure the pain of childbirth. Worrying about stretch marks was not needed. No dealing with having to lose the weight gained and getting back into shape. No leaky breasts. Pumping my breasts was not necessary. Long nights with little to no sleep during the first few months would not be a problem. Maybe adopting was a blessing after all. I tried to replace the negative looping with a more positive perspective. Just perhaps, these tender mercies along my path to motherhood held their own unspoken blessings.

The important thing was that I would have a family. I would get to be a mom. My dream was coming to fruition. Those experiences would be mine. It felt wonderful to know that I'd be able to join in mothers' conversations and feel a new sense of belonging.

When we finally got our travel date, it was in late May, and I would only miss the last week of school. Still, it was sad knowing I wouldn't get to say goodbye to my students by celebrating the end of the school year with them. Their excitement for me, though, made it easier to let go and look forward to what was ahead. We made our airline reservations to Ethiopia, leaving San Francisco in the late afternoon and connecting through Los Angeles and Frankfurt for a layover, before finally landing in Addis Ababa early in the morning almost two days later. We would meet with an adoption guide at the airport to be taken to our hotel, which had already been reserved.

The Joint Council on International Children's Services (JCICS) and IAN discourage parents from staying in Ethiopia between the court and embassy (visa) appointments. We were asked to sign an extended stay agreement. There is no guaranteed time frame. The embassy is required to complete an 1604 investigation before the visa is issued to verify the child's status as an orphan before the processing of the immigrant visa. The agreement stated that the process would not be expedited in any way. We would be expected to be on our best behavior and follow the Cultural Sensitivity Policy. This agreement released IAN of any liability if something were to go wrong. They wanted us to understand that an extended stay in Ethiopia can be physically, mentally, and emotionally demanding for all travelers. We signed it, undeterred by the warnings. We understood the risks, but our determination outweighed any hesitation. Despite the cautions, we chose to push forward—insisting on staying as long as it took, no matter what we might face.

Our travel date had finally arrived, and we were all packed and ready to go. Hue arrived to drive us to the San Francisco airport. Everything was in place, and our neighbors would be taking care of our house plants and pets. Airline tickets, passports, and Visas—check. Money, bills paid, phones, and iPad—check. Mail on hold, toys and books, baby clothes, diapers, and bottles, James and Dad. Check, check, check. Mom? There I stood with a plethora of fear and hesitation flooding my brain. I laid down on the couch and could not move.

I began crying and my friend Hue came over to me to see what was going on. I told her I wasn't sure I could do this. I had a great life with my husband and son in a great home. Everything was about to change. What if my life was ruined? What if this was all a mistake? I could not follow through with this. Hue looked at me and said, "This is what you wanted! You worked hard for this! Those girls are waiting for you and you need to get up off that couch and come with me now!" I didn't realize it at the time, but this was the beginning of what is called Post Adoption Depression (PAD)—a very real and often unexpected emotional struggle that can affect adoptive parents. Even when a child is deeply wanted and anticipated, overwhelming worry, doubt, and grief can set in as the magnitude of change becomes real. I had read a paper about this from the adoption agency a few years ago while working on our first adoption, but had forgotten that it was an actual "thing." Her words helped me realize, at that point, just how much I had wanted this. I felt ashamed of myself for feeling so overwhelmed, but finally got up and went with them.

By the time we arrived at the airport I was back on board to begin this journey to Ethiopia. We had one-way tickets and no known date as to when we would return. Just the knowledge of it taking at least two months and possibly up to five, was daunting. More than anything, it was the unknown that got to me most. It was Thursday afternoon, and we were scheduled to arrive on Saturday early morning. We were off on our adventure. The three of us. A growing family.

Section 5

Ethiopia Abroad:
An Authentic Journal

Within these pages are my honest, day-to-day experiences living far from home as my family grew. Through these candid entries, I invite you to join me in the uncertainty, laughter, hopes, and challenges of our journey to bring our girls home.

Chapter 15

We landed in Ethiopia on schedule, relieved that the many flights behind us had gone smoothly. Stepping off the plane, I was hit with a surge of exhaustion and disorientation that so often accompanies so many hours in the air. Still, beneath the fatigue, there was a restless anticipation—realizing that the real journey was just beginning.

After we collected our luggage and went through customs, we stepped outside. The weather was sunny, yet cooler than Sacramento. We waited at the curb for about thirty minutes, hoping our ride would show—jet lag weighing heavily on me as annoyance and a touch of nervousness crept in. Navigating the first moments in a foreign country without a familiar face to meet us was unsettling. When it became clear no one was coming, we called the adoption agency. They said they would try to reach someone, but with no idea how long that would take, we decided to get the hotel address and grab a taxi. Not exactly a reassuring welcome, but we just wanted to get settled.

I was hoping this was just a hiccup and not indicative of what was to be expected. When we arrived at the hotel, it was still early and our room was not ready, so we ordered some breakfast while we waited. The restaurant was attached to the hotel. It was a spacious room with burgundy carpets and drapes. There was a large mahogany bar and only a few customers spread out in the restaurant. The ambiance was nice and helped us to relax while we waited for someone from the agency to arrive. Eventually our adoption guide showed up, and we were escorted to our room. Throughout the day we tried to rest and get over our jet lag. Every so often we could hear the call to prayer and prayers coming from outside at the nearby mosque. I wasn't sure if the prayers were being spoken in Arabic or Amharic. But it was a very melodious sound, and although we were trying to sleep, it was a relaxing murmur.

Our room at the Addis View Hotel was rather small, but fairly comfortable. The bathroom was a bit tight though. I wasn't sure how we would be able to share the space with all five of us. But that was the least of my concerns right then. Our hearts were nearly bursting with anticipation and joy, knowing that we were just a day away from finally meeting the twins who would complete our family. We would be meeting them the next day at the children's center where they lived. I was very relieved to have a night to rest and get over the jet lag so we could be fully present and fresh when we finally met our daughters.

Excitement buzzed through the morning as we prepared for the moment we traveled so far for—the chance to meet our girls at the IAN care center. Visiting hours were limited: we were allowed to see them either between 9 and 11 a.m. or 3 and 5 p.m., only two-hour intervals permitted each day. We would arrive at the afternoon visiting time.

Once we arrived at the care center, a caregiver quietly led the three of us upstairs to the nursery—the place where we would finally meet our daughters. My heart beat wildly as we stepped into the brightly lit room, lined with about twenty cribs. A small kitchenette stood at the back, sunlight warming the deep red carpet underfoot. Each child had a crib of their own. Two young women caregivers moved quietly among the children.

And then I saw them: Marta, the little girl we would name Eliza, was sitting in a Bumbo seat, tiny and attentive, meeting our gaze with wide, searching eyes. Just a few feet away in her crib was Merma, who would soon become our Zoey, holding a small toy close to her chest. Eliza and Zoey. My breath caught at the sight of them—so close and yet separated. I wondered how often they were given time together, these sisters about to discover what it means to be family. It was another surreal moment in my life. I was meeting my daughters for the first time at eight-and-a-half months old. They were sweeter than pie. I was in heaven, and these were my little angels. Our beautiful family was finally together.

Then the email chain began with my friend who was planning to stay in Ethiopia for the duration of her adoption, Andrea. She had already adopted her son a couple weeks prior and had a chance to meet our girls at the orphanage. I was hoping to meet up and have a support system through the time we would live in Ethiopia. It would be good to stay social and have friends during this wonderful, yet stressful time.

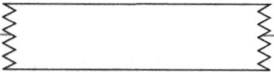

From: Barbara Robertson Horner

Sent: Sunday, June 2, 2013

To: Andrea

Andrea,

We are at the Addis View. IAN did not set up our reservation, and no one arrived at the airport to meet us. We took a taxi to hotel. Met the girls today. I think they love us already :-). Where are you staying?

Barbara

To: Barbara Robertson Horner

Sent: Sunday, Jun 2, 2013

Barbara,

Oh dear lord - that is unfortunately not at all uncommon.

I'm staying out in the Nefas Silk area which is code for far away, but I'd love to meet up with you guys for lunch or dinner some day this week if you're available. I'm so sorry that your arrival was bumpy but SUPER glad that you've met your girls - we LOOOOOVED them!

Let me know when is good for you. Email is a little spotty so best to call or text if you can (the front desk can help you if you don't have your own Ethiophone).

Would you like to go to Serenades? It's by the National Museum in the Piazza. Or Lucy's Gazebo at the National Museum?

Andrea

While we were adopting in Vietnam, I had an iPod to entertain myself. That was the cool new tech next to the iPhone, which had just been invented, but out of my price range. But now it was 2013 and I had an iPad. This invention had only been out for a couple years by then, and I was excited to have one for journaling and to be able to FaceTime my family.

The following pages are taken directly from my journal during our time in Ethiopia—raw and honest, with a few added details for clarity. As I reread these words, I'm reminded of just how daunting those days were. The unknown stretched ahead of us, and the fear and uncertainty often felt overwhelming. But amidst all of that. I still found joy and a sense of humor that got me through it all. This was life as I experienced it, moment by moment.

6/3/13

We have met or seen about ten European couples staying at the Addis View who are here adopting as well. One couple (he, German and she, Spanish) adopted a 5/6-year-old boy who is having some issues (one of which is epileptic symptoms-seizures).

Today we went to meet IAN staff for an orientation of what to expect over the course of our trip and to complete required paperwork for the adoption. Our Power of Attorney was K. Getachew to represent us and act as our agent in our name, place, and stead to locate, identify, and process paperwork of children, upon our consent through IAN for the purpose of adoption such as:

- Represent us with the Ethiopian Government and/or private agencies. organizations, and courts
- Represent us with the Embassy of the United States of America
- Prepare and sign all documents on behalf of us and the children to be adopted by us

- Secure medical testing on the children
- Make applications for and obtaining birth certificates, passports, visas
- Appoint persons to assist in adoption process and childcare
- To delegate third part whenever necessary

We had to agree and sign with a notary. Our court date was scheduled the next day. We were then taken to turn in paperwork and pay for girls' visas at the IAN office. Learned about Court and what questions they ask... Court is tomorrow at 2:00 p.m. Once we pass court, the girls are legally ours and we can take custody of them. Within a few days the court will complete their new birth certificates naming us as the parents, and court decree. IAN will issue our paperwork to Embassy next Wednesday. Learned that it could be as soon as 15 days to Embassy when the visas are processed and issued. Then we can go home.

Visited twins for two hours at the orphanage. They were sleeping when we arrived. Zoey awoke first within 15 minutes. Ten minutes later, Ellie awoke. They ate porridge. We played and held them. Tomorrow we will visit again in a.m.

Noticed the bigger kids do have small rooms off of the main rooms where their bunks are.

After we spent time with the girls, we were to leave on an IAN sponsored trip to Entoto Mountain which is said to be the best location to observe the panoramic view of Addis Ababa. We were able to see one of the oldest churches in Ethiopia, Maryam (St. Mary) Church in these gorgeous mountains, which was built by Emperor Menelik in 1877. Several articles of historical significance were on display, that had been donated by members of the royal family, diplomats, and individuals, in the Menelik Museum. The architectural design and the inner wall paintings of the church are quite captivating. We also visited the Menelik Palace and Mausoleum. It was lovely to be learning some of the history of Ethiopia. The most fascinating site for me though was watching the women fuel wood carriers who would carry Eucalyptus firewood down the mountain on their backs. Some of the piles carried were larger than the woman carrying it. These were strong and tenacious women.

6/4/13

Our Court Day. Family Court Trip Checklist: 1600, notarized (one per child, plus one extra), Privacy Act Waiver, notarized, Child's Embassy Visa Fee ($230 per child) – all to be put in an envelope clearly marked with our family name – and copies of each, Passports, clothes, diapers, bottles, and formula.

Awoke to chanting again. James and I got up at 5. He played Mickey Mouse Clubhouse on the iPad, while I meditated. The IAN Ethiopian staff picked us up from the hotel at 8:30 AM. This day was very exciting, yet I felt nervous. Went to visit twins at 9:30 a.m. They were very happy. We blew bubbles for them. They seemed only slightly interested. James blew bubbles for some older kids—older than him—and they had a blast chasing and popping them. They then played together throwing stuffed animals and laughing. James makes friends everywhere we go. Almost all the strangers on the street stare and smile at him. Many make contact either by giving high fives or rubbing his head. At the hotel they pick him up and kiss him. He is a good sport about it. He says, "Everybody likes me." They think he is beautiful and they love touching his soft, black, shiny hair.

Zoey fell asleep in my arms and when I tried to lay her down in her crib, she instantly awoke and cried for me to pick her up again. James seemed to bond with her the first two days and today he connected with Eliza. He is very pleased they both respond positively to him. I did not want to leave the girls today.

We went to a pizzeria for lunch. Pretty tasty. Bekele* picked us up at 1:10 and we went to the office to pick up Aisha, our lawyer. Next stop, Court. Originally, we were to meet the twin's birth parents, but this was not to be since they could not be found. The court was much more relaxed than I had anticipated. We had dressed professionally, although the atmosphere was more friendly than overly formal. It was a lovely and comfortable experience unlike the court adoption in Vietnam.

The court waiting room was packed with Europeans waiting to adopt. We got called first and were told we were not next. Back out into the waiting area. One by one couples were called in and would return teary-eyed with joy that they had passed court. Not that there was any question that we would pass, but it was reassuring. Finally, after about ten couples, we were called in to the judge's chambers. She asked about ten questions, such as "Have you visited the twins? Have you taken courses on international adoption? Do you plan to keep the girls in touch with their Ethiopian culture? Are you sure you want to continue with the adoption?" She then announced we were the legal parents and there was no turning back. This is when I finally felt emotion and teared up. She then apologized for not giving us much eye contact because she was so taken by James. She loved the way he sounded when he talked. James did well and gets chocolate and Angry Birds Star Wars play time when we get back to the hotel :-).

Hell yeah! We were accepted as the adoptive family and the adoption was finalized. We could now take Marta and Merma to live with us at our guest house; however, we did not get the girls because Michael wanted to wait for the paperwork to be completed. I asked the lawyer about the timeline and realized it could be longer than I was okay with leaving our daughters in the orphanage. After further discussion with Mike, we agreed to arrange to pick up the girls tomorrow. Yeah!!! This was a huge relief, but the more daunting wait was still to come.

* Bekele was our appointed chauffeur.

6/5/13

Today we picked up the girls from the care center. They would now live with us for the next eighteen years! I brought some cute clothes to put on them for their new life with their new family. We thanked the women for their loving care and left. We went back to our guest house/hotel with our newly adopted twin girls in tow. The room seemed even smaller now that there were five of us. We had the manager send up two small cribs for us and the space got even smaller. After I fed and put the kids down for a nap, I got onto my email and tried to locate Andrea who had arrived three weeks earlier. I told her where we were and she insisted that we come stay at The Afro Land Lodge where she was staying with her family. We met up with them the next day for dinner at an outdoor restaurant near where we were staying. We really enjoyed our visit and decided that the Afro Land Lodge sounded more hospitable for us if we were to be living in Ethiopia for a few months. They had suites with king bed and infant cribs, a small kitchen, larger bathroom, living room, TV, and breakfast served in your room each morning. The breakfast in the room sounded wonderful. We wouldn't have to get everyone dressed just to eat.

To: Barbra Robertson Horner

Sent: Wednesday, June 5, 2013

Barbara,

Are you guys still here? If you are, do you want to meet up for lunch or dinner before you head home?

Andrea

————————————————————————-

From: Barbara Robertson Horner

Sent: Wednesday, Jun 5, 2013

Andrea,

We are here for the duration of the adoption. We passed court and we have custody of our twin girls. When would you like to meet up? We are available Tomorrow if that works for you.

Barbara

To: Barbara Robertson Horner

Sent: Wednesday, June 5, 2013

Barbara,

Tomorrow - yes! Where and when?

Andrea

6/6/13

Day two with the girls and we wake up to no water. Now this may seem like a minor problem to some, but the implications upon further inspection are huge. Consider we are dealing with babies here. You know, those cute little cherubs that giggle and laugh, smile and babble, cuddle and love, and yes, eat, pee, and poop. The latter being something where water comes in handy. Anyhow, we are made to buy bottled water from the hotel. Seems odd that the hotel, upon registration, offered water as one of the amenities, would turn around and charge for bottled water. Apparently, the government was to blame. I guess it's the same all over the world. When in trouble, blame the government. So we proceed through the day.

Before coming to Ethiopia, I had begun email correspondence with another woman who was also adopting from Ethiopia. She and her husband live in Orlando, Florida and are also three+ years into another adoption, from China. They received their referral in December as well. The adoption agency had connected all the December families in case they wanted to communicate. Andrea and I connected and we decided to meet up in Addis Ababa. She was planning to stay through Embassy, which is what encouraged us to decide to do the same. She and her husband had arrived two weeks prior to us and had some good insights to share. Yeah!!

We were to meet at Serenade's Restaurant at 5 p.m. Upon arrival the restaurant was not yet serving- the sign said 3 p.m.- 9 p.m.- although their posted hours and hours of operation where two different moments in time. Speaking of time, did I mention the clocks in Addis Ababa? There are clocks everywhere we go, and most of them run; however, they all tout different times, none of which match the standard satellite time for this time zone (on this planet). Luckily, Andrea's family was late, and I was able to borrow our driver's phone to call her. After three dropped calls, we connected. She was having difficulty finding the place-it is off the beaten path. We decided to meet at Lucy's Gazebo instead.

Andrea arrived with her 13-month-old son, Permera, and her friend from the states. Her husband had already returned home to work. We had a lovely dinner. It was nice to be able to speak fluent English with someone other than my husband. She had found an English-speaking European pediatrician that she recommended- good to know. They had just found a nice place to stay in the Bole district. We were looking to move soon to a place that was quieter and less expensive. The description sounded great and being near a support person sounded fabulous. We planned to check it out. Back at the hotel and still no water. I wish I had bathed the girls yesterday when we got them. I just assumed... Our driver assured us the water would be back on by morning.

From: Barbara Robertson Horner

Sent: Thursday, June 6, 2013

Andrea,

Wherever you like. I haven't been to any of those places yet.

Would you like to meet for early dinner or late lunch? How about 5 o'clock?

 Barbar*a*

—————————————————————-

To: Barbara Robertson Horner

Sent: Thursday, June 6, 2013

Barbara,

We'll head your way whenever is good for you. Putting Premara down for a nap in about a half an hour until noon. Maybe after then? 5 would be great!

Andrea

I'll be the one who looks exhausted :)

Andrea

From: Barbara Robertson Horner

Sent: Thursday, June 6, 2013

Andrea,

Okay five it is. See you at Serenades restaurant at 5 p.m. today.

Barbara

———————————————————————-

To: Barbara Robertson Horner

Sent: Thursday, June 6, 2013

Barbara,

We'll be there! I'll be the one who looks exhausted :)

Andrea

6/7/13

Someday we will get to sleep again... Hallelujah, no water again- sarcasm. Okay, this is not going to work! Twin babies, a five-year-old, and two spoiled American adults who care about hygiene. I refuse to eat in the hotel restaurant, I don't care if breakfast is included. No water, no washing of hands. I don't know about you, but I like to think the person preparing my food has washed their hands. Hard to imagine this is the case in a restaurant with no water. No coffee or tea. Grumpy and grumpier are checking out of this Popsicle stand. Mike had called Kelile* a couple days ago regarding checking on some guest houses. He called him again this morning to let him know that we needed to move to a new place today. Bekele would be available to drive us to a couple places to check out. So we packed and got the hell out of Dodge.

When Bekele showed up, we let him know about the guest house where Andrea was staying. He was familiar with the Afro Land Lodge, so he took us there first. The hotel clerk showed us two options: one small suite for $55 per night, and a larger suite for $70. The larger suite included a queen bed, living room, T.V., Internet, full bath, kitchen area, a shared cooking kitchen, and breakfast included. They wanted to charge $15 extra per crib, and we negotiated the cribs included at no extra cost. All this, plus running water–ha! It was more than we wanted to spend, but less than the Addis View and far superior. Being able to cook our own food will save us money and heartburn. Sold! We took the larger room. Sometimes comfort is worth paying extra- especially in this situation. We have spent almost 40 grand on this adoption process, what's a few more dollars for creature comforts.

 So we took our bags upstairs, made the girls' bottles, and hopped back in the van with Bekele. He took us to a grocery to buy some provisions. After choosing a few items, I realized we didn't have enough birr to pay. The grocery store didn't take credit cards or dollars, as is the case for most merchants in Addis Ababa (as we were discovering). I exchanged twenty dollars for birr with our driver. We went to the van, and the clerk came running out of the store claiming a mistake had been made, and we owed them more money. A bunch of words in Amharic were exchanged, and the driver handed him some more money. Still confused about what exactly went down.

Next stop, the mall. We were dropped off to do some shopping. Suppos- edly a place that took credit cards. Bekele would return in two hours. We went up to a cafe to get lunch first. Mike asked the server if they accept credit cards, and she said yes—finding out later that yes is the standard response when we are not understood. As we were sitting at the table, I unhooked the Bjorne and discovered that Zoey (my diarrhea queen) had another episode—this time it blew out the back of her diaper and all over the Bjorne. Holy crap! Literally. So I ran to the bathroom with her. Reminder, third world country, Koala Bear changing stations are non-existent. I had to lay her on the floor of the bathroom. As soon as I removed the diaper, she streamed pee all over the edge of

the Bjorne and the floor. I quickly moved her up higher onto the Bjorne, grabbed the blanket I was using, and sopped up the urine. At that exact moment she let loose again and created her own Crater Lake in the center of the Bjorne. Good thing they are absorbent. At this point I am about ready to lose it and exchange this baby for a one-way ticket home. No, really. What ever happened to 'cute and cuddly.' So I pull myself together and returned to the restaurant somewhat disheveled. I collect my composure and exchanged babies for fear she would blow out her onesie.

After we finished eating, the credit card was placed in the bill folder and picked up by our server. She quickly returned to inform us that they did not take credit cards. This was the same woman who told us before we sat down that they did take credit cards. So I have no birr to pay, and they don't take dollars. The manager then comes out to solve the dilemma. After a slight communication breakdown, he walks me downstairs to a bank so that I can exchange my dollars for birr and pay the bill. Once I arrived back at the restaurant and paid the bill, Eliza needed a diaper change. I again lay a baby on a receiving blanket on the bathroom floor, remove the diaper and experience Niagara Falls. I can't believe it happened again. One more time, I sop up the urine with the blanket. What did I ever do to deserve this? I swear at this point the Powers that be are testing me. Either that, or I'm being followed by Ethiopia's version of Candid Camera.

Off we go to shop. No one takes credit cards. I am trying to make my cash last, and at this rate I am afraid I will run out before trip's end. We realize that there is no more time to shop anyway. Does not matter, at this point I am eager to return to the hotel. The day's end is not soon enough.

 * Kelile was our in country coordinator.

6/8/13

I have decided that it might be best to chill with the girls at the hotel for a few days until we have gotten into a routine and understand each other better. So, Mike and James can venture out without us to run errands and explore. Quality guy time. I feel I need to really work on bonding with the girls. It's been a rough ride so far and I fear I am suffering from PAD (Post adoption depression). Almost three years leading up to the screaming and pooping twins—think I'll go online and read some self-help literature. Before we got here, I worried about the girls bonding with us—did not anticipate that I would be the one who would have the issue.

Mike went downstairs to cook some dinner while the four of us hung out in the room. I have discovered over the past four days that Zoey is my squirter (probably due to the anxiety of her new transition into our family) and Eliza is a bit constipated—for the same reason. So anyway, Zoey is on the couch with her big brother, who is playing a video game on the iPad, and Ellie starts to get that glazed look in her eyes and starts to cry. She is trying to push out one of her rocks, so I rush her into the bathroom and sit her on the toilet, encouraging her to drop the biscuit. Meanwhile, Zoey starts screaming and at this point Ellie has already started her evacuation. I call out to James to play with her and he says okay. But she continues to scream. James claims nothing is wrong. He is playing with her. I call out again for him to stop playing the video game and play with his sister. He says, "Okay Mom." She continues to scream. I ask James what is wrong, and he says, "Nothing."

"Then why is she screaming?"

"I don't know?"

Finally, Eliza is done with her dirty deed. I rush out to the living room to find my 5-year-old still playing a video game and Zoey rolling in the diarrhea that squirted out all over the coach. I quickly grab Zoey, lay her in the bathtub, throw a diaper on Ellie (who then starts screaming when I desert her for Zoey). So now I have two screaming babies, a husband rushing through the door to see what all the screaming's about, and a five-year-old who is being scolded and claiming he was playing with the baby and didn't know she had defecated...

To: Barbara Robertson Horner

Sent: Saturday, June 8, 2013,

Barbara,

Did James receive his package yet? Please let me know when you get it.

Love you,

Becky

From: Barbara Robertson Horner

Sent: Saturday, June 8, 2013

Becky,

This is where we will be living the remainder of the time:

Afro Land Lodge
Gabon Road, Bole Sub-city
Addis Ababa, Ethiopia

I tried to let them know at the hotel that we were expecting a package. But we left upset because there was no water for two days. And we did not know where we're going. So we will let Abdi know and asked him to call the hotel.

Barbara

6/9/13

James is pretty well inundated with an eczema rash that started yesterday and has spread ten-fold. The guys plan to heed my warnings that James should eat nothing that might, even remotely, contain milk. This is James' first full-fledged outbreak since he was an infant. He now gets my diligence to keep him from consuming the allergen. Poor guy. For all intents and purposes, we will stick with plant foods.

Milk is incorporated into most restaurant foods here. Now that we are staying in a hotel where we can cook our own foods, we will be able to control what ingredients James eats. There is a fresh fruit and vegetable stand just outside our hotel. Also, Mike found a bakery that bakes breads with just grains (whole grains), water, and salt. He also found a store close by that sells whole grain pasta. Up to this point, we have only encountered white bread and pastas. The little things get us so excited. Speaking of little things, Zoey is now rolling over on her own, and both girls are having less-stressed bowel movements. When one is hotel bound, these little things become the topic of interest. A couple more days and we can go on another venture as a family—still recovering from the last one.

6/10/13

Indian take-out, vegan, takes Visa, asked for not spicy, got spicy, poor James. Did find freshly baked whole grain barley bread sticks. Yum!

Twins are finally adjusting to the 8-month-old schedule I found online.

James is adjusting to big brotherhood. Mom is still having a difficult time letting go of her little boy.

6/11/13

Retail therapy day. We went shopping where Services Along the Nile Ethiopia textiles made by blind artisans are sold. I bought some cute stuffed hippos, a stuffed giraffe, and Christmas angel ornaments...

6/13/13

9:15 in the morning and the telephone rings. We had just finished breakfast and put the girls down for their morning nap when the phone rang. It was the hotel receptionist calling to let us know that Bekele was downstairs. We were a bit perplexed considering we were not expecting him. Mike went down to receive him, and unbeknownst to us, he had arrived to take us to get the twins vaccinated. No forewarning, it was time to go. He was kind enough to give us 15 minutes to get our family of five ready.

So we got the three kids dressed, teeth brushed, bottles made, diaper bag packed, and ourselves presentable, all in 15 minutes. Record! Immunizations here we come. The hard part for us is that we are not big fans of vaccines. But when you are adopting from a foreign and developing country, you don't want to ruffle anyone's feathers. Can't get the kids passports and visas in a timely manner without complying with the rules. Just go with the flow and let me get the hell out of here with my babies. We all pack into Bekele's van, Andrea and her son as well, and head toward a medical center in some back-alley place where we are turned away because the vaccinations are not being distributed that day. Which is fine with us because the place looked a bit sketchy and several sickly-looking people with their children were sitting outside in the "courtyard." The journey for vaccines continues.

We arrived at the next medical clinic, ironically to be greeted by a huge cloud of exhaust. This place was handing out shots, so we cued up and waited our turn. The whole experience was extremely surreal. We walked up two flights of stairs, being stared at by everyone we passed, and sat down next to a woman breastfeeding her baby. Soon we were escorted into a room for weighing the babies. Both weighed 9 kg. (translation, about 19.8 lbs.) although I swear Zoey is heavier.

Then onward to the vaccination room. This room had a doctor at a desk recording information, and a nurse delivering the vaccine (measles, mumps, and rubella). Although the sign on the wall claimed the supplies in the boxes included gloves, there were none in sight and the vaccines were given one right after another with no break for any sanitation, i.e., alcohol wash, hand wash, or gloves. Just a fresh needle thrown into an open can after use. The girls did well, only a few short tears (so much less dramatic than when James was vaccinated in Vietnam). Then the doctor proceeded to tell us, three times, that we needed to get the girls immunized again in December and every six months until they are five. We nodded in agreement and smiled.

Previous to our arrival, the girls had received their other shots, so now all the vaccines have been given.

Next stop is a requested visit to the IAN office. Michael needed to get the court decree stating we adopted the girls so he can mail it to Family Leave to receive paternity compensation. Also, it's a good idea to carry it while enjoying the local culture with kids in tow, just in case the local police stop and question the legitimacy of your parenthood of children who do not look like you.

When we arrived at the office, the whole crew was there to meet us. While exchanging hellos, I asked politely when we would be getting our passport pictures, and Kelile said we could do it today if the girls' outfits were okay for the pictures. I just laughed and said, "I didn't think they would mind." I was just happy to get one more procedure checked off the list of "getting us home sooner." So the girls got their pictures taken right there in the office. Had I not asked, I don't think it would have occurred to them to have offered. Strange days indeed. Mike also asked Kelile if he could give us a heads up before upcoming appointments so that we are sure to be available and not out and about taking in the culture. He agreed.

Later that afternoon, there was a knock at the door. It was the manager, a well-dressed, nice-looking gentleman who is very cordial. He had paid us a visit two days ago to let us know the construction going on next door had unintentionally broke the waterline and we would need to conserve since the hotel had only a small backup tower for such events. It was nice to have an upfront communication (compared to the lack thereof at the Addis View). Well, he was the bearer of unfortunate news once again, only the city was turning off the water supply for half the city in efforts to build the train system that was being developed through town, only this time it would be for three days, possibly longer—starting this afternoon. I thanked him for his candidness in imparting this information. He apologized for the inconvenience and left.

I guess we can't run away from the water problems. It seems to be following us. Before coming to Addis Ababa we had learned it is a good idea to bring flashlights due to intermittent power outages; however, the water turn offs were a bit of a surprise. The only electrical issues have been short lived, a few seconds to a few minutes in duration. Fingers crossed the water gets turned on sooner than later.

6/14/13

A few days ago, a couple from Canada (packing up to go back home to Edmonton with their baby boy) gave us the number of their driver, Meleak (who just happens to live in the compound below our window). He came highly recommended for his integrity and fair price. So yesterday, Mike called him and arranged for him to take us around town to do some cultural shopping. He offered his services for 400 birr (~$20), which included being our tour guide, driving us to a scarf factory, the Mercado, the best coffee in Ethiopia, and a return trip back to the hotel. Andrea would accompany us and split the cost. What a deal. At noon we all crammed into his blue Lada (two adults and four kids in the back, and Mike in the front—kids aren't allowed in the front, and only the driver has a working seat belt). Addis Ababa here we come.

The first stop was in Kolfe, a sub city of Addis Ababa, where the scarf factory is located. Inside the building are several looms. On the day we arrived, only four weavers were at work. Each weaver produces two scarves per day. The weavers offered to let us try, but honestly it looked too complicated for my rearing twins in a hotel in Addis Ababa mind. James wanted to try, only his legs were too short for the pedals. They let him turn a crank though and he was quite happy with that. We then went into the shop next door to purchase some scarves. The scarves were priced at 70 birr each (roughly $3.75 each). They are very beautiful. We bought several as gifts. So much work for such little money. I felt a bit guilty not paying more.

On our way back to the car we did some shopping at the open market that we had to walk past. Bought some cultural dresses for the twins, jewelry, some knitted hats, and a scarf that says "I Love Ethiopia." Feeling the touristy thing now. Donkeys, merchants calling us in, tall lady with a twig in her nose, begging children, pulling my purse close. Time to go to the Mercado. The Mercado is a district of merchants that sell traditional and cultural wares, including spices. It is so vast and a great place to do some bargain shopping (negotiating). Definitely a place to visit more than once—especially when lugging around small children. Again, merchants calling us in, begging children, pulling my purse close.

Meleak was so great, he would help us haggle. After a while, I was getting a better deal than he was. He even helped carry our merchandise. The last stop was for some amazing Ethiopian coffee at Caffe Tomoca. Beans are roasted on sight. Michael and Andrea each ordered a double Macchiato. I am not a coffee drinker, but I tried a taste of Mike's and had to order one for myself. I am glad I ordered a single because I was flying high with a caffeine buzz. So Yummy! Best coffee I've ever encountered. I could become addicted to coffee if I had access to this place every day. Move over Starbucks! Had to buy some beans for gifts.

Headed back to the hotel. Crazy driving through a town with no traffic signals, no crosswalks, pedestrians dodging cars, and cars dodging pedestrians, in a car with no seat belts once again. Hold those babies close.

6/15/13

Water is back on :-).

Afro Land is really much better than our last hotel. It is nice to have a family we know living upstairs from us. The staff is lovely as well. We settled right in and James made friends with the manager and the woman who works the front desk. He is only five, but very social. They think he is adorable. He has a friendly demeanor and shiny straight black hair that makes people want to stroke it. It is so different than their wooly, curly afros and braids. He was taken aback by the hair stroking when a stranger on the street touched his shiny mane but has grown to expect it however annoying it is.

(Later in the U.S. my girls would come to realize a similar annoyance with White people wanting to touch their "unique" hair.)

There are several commodities nearby. There is a small open market that sells fresh vegetables and fruit where we can buy bananas and avocados - easy baby food, a bank for exchanging currency, a bakery for bread and treats, and a larger grocery store a few blocks away where we can buy diapers, formula, pasta, and cheese, called Friendship Supermarket.

Meleak, the taxi driver, is super knowledgeable about how to get around the construction bound city with limited signage, stop lights and paved roads. (This is a city being built almost everywhere we went.) He was friendly, dependable, and honest. All the things you hope for in a taxi driver. He loves our families and we love him. James also became fast friends with him and got to sit on his lap and steer the driving wheel while they drove around the block.

Our daily ritual starts with a delicious breakfast with juice, coffee, and tea. I was not a coffee drinker when we arrived in Ethiopia, but I enjoyed tea with milk. We would play, bathe, watch T.V., read, write, and nap. We would also make plans occasionally with Andrea, Frank, and their child who is a few months older than our twins, but from the same orphanage. He has beautiful dark brown skin that is almost black in color and they have kept his birth name. We on the other hand renamed our girls; Marta was now Eliza and Merma was now Zoey. They are not identical so it is easy to tell them apart. Our plans usually consist of daily excursions to places around the city where we can eat and shop. Sometimes we visit parks and tourist attractions. Andrea and I would joke that we needed to go out and get some retail therapy just to have something to do besides sitting in our guest house and waiting to hear from the IAN Ethiopian staff for our social, medical, and visa trips. We were not allowed to leave the city because there are no set dates and we need to be available when appointments are set and available. Often at the last minute.

Some days we like to have our taxi friend just drive us around until we see something of interest, but usually we find places in our Lonely Planet guidebook or in the brochures for the Federal Democratic Republic of Ethiopia Ministry of Culture and Tourism Authority For Research & Conservation of Cultural Heritage (that is the longest title I've ever seen).

A place that we were interested in going to today was the National Museum of Ethiopia... so Andrea's family and our family took a trip there.

The main attraction was Lucy, the skeletal remains, actually 47 bones, one of the earliest human ancestors from the species Australopithecus afarensis. This discovery had taken place when I was nine and I remembered seeing it in the news, however, I had learned about this paleontological find in more detail when I took an anthropology class in college and was excited to actually see it in person. The skeleton had been found in Ethiopia, thus its location at the National Museum of Ethiopia.

There were three levels above the paleoanthropological exhibits in the basement of the museum. On the first level there are ancient, medieval, and royal artifacts. On the second floor there are various art forms throughout time in Ethiopian culture, and the third being mostly more ethnographic history and studies. Ethiopia being one of the oldest nations and what scientists call the cradle of civilization makes this a must see place to visit while in Addis Ababa.

6/16/13

We were planning to go to a national soccer game today, Ethiopia vs. South Africa, but Kelile called us last night and invited us to his son's birthday party (six years old). We felt obligated to go since he is the in country coordinator and we want to stay on his good side. He mentioned that other adopting couples from the U.S.A. would be there as well—a good opportunity to network and compare experiences with IAN. Bekele arrived at noon to pick us up, Andrea and her son too. It was about a 35-minute drive. Along the way we saw several people wearing the Ethiopia colors (red, green, and yellow), some with painted faces and flags, preparing celebrations for the big game. Truck loads, van loads, and even bus loads all decked out. Great spirit!

When we arrived at Kelile's, we were greeted by his three children. His place was very middle class per Ethiopian standards. He had a lovely garden and yard. His house was modest yet sturdy, set up in a more western motif than Ethiopian ethnic. Two couples from the U.S.A. had already arrived, one from Indianapolis, and the other from Atlanta-both in their late twenties.

We sat down at the table with them. Kelile offered beverages: Coke, Mirinda, St. George Beer, Meta Beer, and water. Then the food began to take over the table. It was a magnificent spread of traditional Ethiopian food. There was light and dark brown injera, salad, seasoned spinach, cheese, brown rice, herbed rice, several lamb dishes and bread. We all chatted and ate, using the injera as utensils. Later, another couple, from Scottsdale, Arizona stopped by. They brought their son whom they adopted from Guatemala a few years ago. They were in the process of a second adoption when Guatemala closed. Thus, they switched to Ethiopia. Kelile's wife came out to make an appearance and welcome us. Some of Kelile's friends hung out in the living room and patio. The kids, including James, played soccer outside.

Upon talking to Melissa (from Indiana), we found out that our adoption agent from IAN in the U.S.A. had walked out on her job on Friday. Not surprised from our correspondence over the past few months. I sensed she was unhappy with her job, having not followed through with her word to take care of business and then getting defensive when confronted or reminded. This could end up being a good thing if we are assigned a new and improved agent to handle our case.

Just after an hour of chit chat and gorging ourselves, the van was ready to take us back to our hotel. This time it was an Addis View driver and he was taking everyone, us first. It seemed a bit odd that we were being escorted out so soon. I suppose it was more a nice gesture than a truly comfortable invite. For now, I'll just leave it at that. On the way back, we witnessed even more people preparing and showing spirit for the soccer game that would be starting in just over an hour.

After we got back to the hotel and rested the kids, we walked over to the Back Porch (with Andrea and son) to watch the second half of the game. The place was packed, so we headed for Bruno's. The place was empty except for staff, and the game was on. We ordered pizza, fries, and beer and watched Ethiopia win the game to advance to the World Cup. Screams and cheers of joy could be heard within and outside. On our walk back to the Afro Land Lodge, we experienced Ethiopia in Mardi Gras style. Car horns honking, people shouting, music playing, alcohol flowing, and the streets full of fans cheering in celebration of their winning team. It was a bit surreal, and then two women walked by and were speaking Amharic to Zoey. The next thing I know, one of the women was touching Zoey all over her face and her finger slid into my mouth. Super gross. I was disgusted and started spitting on the street (not a typical behavior for me, but all I could think of was where her hands might have been before entering my mouth). As soon as we got back to our room I washed Zoey's face, my mouth, and took three Immunity pills. There's just something about a stranger's hand in your mouth, especially in a city full of homeless and not so clean citizens. The celebrations continued throughout the night.

6/17/13

Today we went to the Addis Ababa Lion Zoo. Not super impressive compared to other zoos where we've been. Safari would probably be better, but we can't leave the city. Several of the lions had black manes unlike the light tan or reddish I am used to seeing.

6/18/13

Today is movie day. Andrea and her son came down with their computer full of movies. I popped some popcorn and Mike cut a watermelon into wedges. We watched Super 8, a suspenseful teen thriller.

6/19/13

It is Wednesday, IAN's day to submit to Embassy. Still have not heard anything regarding immigration status on the girls' passports, or an appointment for their physical. Michael tried to call Kelile a few times yesterday, but no answer. Today though, he was able to reach a social worker at the Ethiopia IAN office. Last Thursday we were told that the immigration paperwork would be submitted that day. This did not occur though. In fact, it had not yet been submitted. She told Michael that the Power of Attorney did not have my name on it, so they could not turn it in. This we knew was not so. Michael asked why we had not been notified all week if this was an issue. She had no response and was apologetic. She said it would have to be fixed, and she would get back to us in an hour.

About an hour and a half later, another social worker showed up at our hotel. He had the birth certificates, court decree, and the adoption contract to show us. Each arrived to them with incomplete names. My middle name was missing, and part of Mike's last name was missing. He said he would take the documents back to the legal entities to be corrected. He said it would take 48 hours and then we could submit to Embassy for the passports. He said we would submit the papers by Friday and it would take 5 business days, then the following Monday, we could take the girls to their medical appointment. Once the medical report is received, they could submit the paperwork to the U.S. Embassy (Wednesdays only) for the visas. The Embassy takes, on average, 15 days to process the visas. Heck, we might be able to leave by July 26th with this timeline. I'm thinking positive and hoping for sooner.

The first three weeks have seemed far longer; now I need to prepare myself for a month and a week longer. I am starting to get why the recommendation is to make two trips. Addis Ababa, Ethiopia is not the most entertaining or easy to get around, especially with three kids in tow. Dinner out for Indian food and drinks may be what the doctor ordered to swallow this pill.

It was starting to rain, so we took a taxi. We went to the Jewel of India with Andrea and her son. The setting was very comfortable. We sat at a table with couches on both sides. Andrea doesn't eat meat either, so we ordered family style. The food was indeed spicy. True authentic Indian cuisine. Very nice. Quite delicious, but we ordered far too much to eat in one sitting. Lunch for tomorrow.

6/20/13

4:50 a.m. and the horner began blowing his horn just outside our hotel. Now I understand that this is the first of six prayer times of each and every day, but this guy was unusually loud and annoying. It scared us out of our very scattered night of sleep. Eliza was up most of the night, and therefore so were we. We are only two blocks from a mosque which broadcasts prayer through its speaker system at 4:51a.m., 6:08 a.m., 12:28 p.m., 3:55 p.m., 6:48 p.m., and 8:01 p.m., give or take a minute depending on the day, and sunrise. One gets used to the chanting, but this guy sounded like a revolution was about to take place.

6/21/13

We received a call from the agency this morning regarding the girls' passports. Apparently, the pictures they took last week in the office were for their birth certificates, not their passports, and we needed to go to the immigration office today to get their passport pictures done. Once again, the communication is lacking. Bekele was to arrive at 2:00 p.m. and arrived at 2:45 p.m. We drove to the immigration office, which was not an impressive building. There were over a hundred people sitting outside on the steps. Makeda led us up the stairs and to one of the entrance gates. We had to push through several people trying to get through the gate. People were waving their papers in hopes of gaining entrance. Makeda led me (holding Zoey) and James through to the other side. Michael (holding Ellie) had to go to the gate on the right side to get in. Once we all entered, we were led into a large room filled with about 200 chairs and about sixty people sitting with sad, despondent eyes and long frowns; some even with tears streaming down their cheeks. The chairs in the room were ripped, the floor was unswept, and quite dirt ridden. The whole room was quite depressing in its lack of cleanliness and design or artwork.

We took our seats at the front near the desk with overflowing wrinkled papers, all which appeared to be the same, possibly application forms that had been filled out. Two men sat at a desk atop a dais. One sat behind while the other sat to the side. They both had grim expressions on their face. The man behind the desk more stern than the other. The men would look at an application and call up the person and then send them to the next room. Because we were adopting children, and because they were under two years of age, we took precedence over the other applicants, which pushed us on through to the next waiting area within 15 minutes. We were again shuffled off, to a corridor, to wait on a bench outside a small room. Several people sat along the benches, while others walked by. A room with windows across from us had a group of about twenty-five people waiting, several staring out at us. I would offer a smile and occasionally receive one back, but mostly very serious, unrelenting grimaces. I'm sure each with a story I could never fathom. After about twenty minutes, we were called in to the room. I was asked to sit down by the desk of the man processing the passports. There was one other desk and two curtains hanging on each side of a room that measured about 8 by 8 feet. The gentleman continued to thumb through all the girls' papers, stamping each one. Then the girls, one at a time, were taken behind the curtain to have their "actual" passport photos taken.

Once that was complete, we went back outside, waited for Makeda to take the papers to the proper authority, and pay the bill.

A few minutes later, she returned and led us out of the immigration compound. When we got back out to the street, Bekele had left,

159

so Makeda got us a taxi. Halfway home, she asked him to stop. She explained she had to get out to go back to her office. She paid the driver and told us not to pay him again when we arrive at the hotel. She then said, "Goodbye, I'll see you on Tuesday for the physical." We were a bit confused, since we were last told that the physical would be Monday of the following week. Next thing we knew, the driver was talking to a police officer. The officer left and returned with Makeda. She paid the driver more money and then left. Not sure what that was all about. I had awoken this morning with a migraine from lack of sleep over the past two nights of Eliza not sleeping. By now my lack of sleep and food today was calling for a walk down to The Back Porch for some comfort food: pizza and French fries. Feeling fatigued!

6/22/13

James mentions going to the park every time we pass by Addis Ababa Park near the President's Palace. So today, we are going to the park to play. Nice weather for it. Andrea's driver is taking us this time. He has a van, so it won't be as cramped as Meleak's Lada. The park is gated and there is an entrance fee. The guards check your bags for cameras when entering. Odd. It is across from the President's Palace, but then I took pictures of the White House, so who knows. It is very clean and the lawn is kept short. The area is long and narrow with water features, one that starts as a big fountain pool at the top of the park that runs down the hill into another pool and continues to flow through the center as a creek. However, all the water was turned off, probably due to the water shortage. Several flowers were in bloom. There are guards who walk the park. About a quarter of the way in from the entrance is a cafe where no one ate while we were there.

There are several structures on which kids can climb, ride, slide, and even a swing. I was climbing a multi-colored metal structure with James and I started hanging upside down when a guard came over and said something to me. I thought he was asking if James was my son, but he kept talking, and he was probably telling me I couldn't be on the structure—I just played dumb since I don't speak Amharic. The twins loved sitting in the grass.

They enjoyed the feel of it and quickly discovered that they could pick it. Zoey, always the eater, was attempting to eat the grass. Soon, Ellie followed suit and began tasting it herself.

James made a friend with a 4 1/2 year old blonde Caucasian boy from Australia. His mother had moved them to Ethiopia for work. Before this, I had not met any White people who lived here. They had fun racing around the park. Great find, and a place we will have to visit several more times.

After the park, Tehut, our driver, took us to the other Tomoca for macchiatos. This one has seats and is placed within a trendy upscale raw meat restaurant. A big slab of a salted beef carcass, Tere Sega, hung on the kitchen wall. This was a place where the wealthier Ethiopians dine and drink. We, all vegetarians, wanted to eat, and while nothing but raw meat was listed on the menu, Michael was able to order us colorful salads and an order of French fries. The macchiato was very good, but the roasting does not take place at this location; the other Tomoca seemed better with the romance of the rustic ambience and the smell of freshly roasted beans wafting through the air.

Next, we drove to a Tuberculosis and Leprosy rehab where they make scarves. Michael wanted to buy some scarves for his coworkers. I felt a bit weird about going, not knowing if we would be in danger of infecting ourselves. When we arrived it was closed. They close at noon. Relief for me.

Tomorrow, Andrea's husband is flying back to Ethiopia from Florida. She is very excited about having him back to help out. We put in an order for a few supplies from the U.S., so we are excited to meet him as well.

6/23/13

Frank has arrived bearing gifts. The dark chocolate was a welcomed indulgence. James especially appreciated the Justin's peanut butter cups.

6/24/13

Received the passports for the girls today. Every milestone is one step closer to being home. ;-)

6/25/13

Another park day planned. Michael is staying back with the girls, and James and I are joining Andrea and her family.

Tehut picked us up at 12:30 and we drove to Addis Ababa Park. It was a bit drizzly off and on, but still nice enough for the kids to enjoy playing. James' Australian friend was there again, this time with his nanny. She confronted me about the function of my uterus, which happens now and again being an adoptive parent. It usually starts with the standard "Do you have any biological children?" or "Do you have any children of your own?", as though my children aren't really mine. If I am patient, I might reply and say no. This sometimes leads into the more intrusive line of questioning, such as, "Are you incapable of having your own...?" Humans are by nature curious beings, but when did my uterus become the topic of conversation with complete strangers. Well, I guess adopting children gives others the license to know about the function of my personal body parts.

After the park, we stopped at Kaldi's coffee shop (a chain), the Starbucks of Ethiopia, even the emblem is a green circle that resembles the Starbucks' emblem. We had been craving ice cream, and did an Internet search. Kaldi's was the only gelato that came up. I must say, it was excellent gelato. What happened next was a series of events that led to an interesting adventure of intrigue and espionage. The coffee shop was located in a small shopping mall, and I left the group in search of baby clothes, which I found on the fourth floor. When I came back downstairs, Frank was standing in the center of the main lobby of the mall with the boys. When I asked where Andrea had gone, he replied that she recognized the IOM (International Organization for Migration) building behind the mall and went over to check the status of a DNA test that she was waiting on, regarding the legitimacy of her son's relationship to the relinquishing birth mother.

She had been calling the IAN office daily since the tests had been done a week prior. She was on them to stay in contact with IOM to check on the results since as soon as the results were in, and cleared her son, the paperwork could be submitted to Embassy for her son's visa. She was on them to do their job and communicate with her, since they had already stalled to let her know that the testing was needed. She arrived May 11th and was ready to get back home as soon as possible. But as we were discovering, IAN has many unnecessary delays due to miscommunication.

We went to find her, and she was coming out of the building. The results were positive. The boy had a match with the birth mom and the medical report and results had been in since last Friday and already submitted electronically to the U.S. Embassy. So she got on her cell phone and called the social worker at IAN. When she answered, Andrea asked her if she had checked with IOM. She claimed she had, and the results were not ready yet. At this point, Andrea called her on the lie and let her know we were at IOM right then and what we had learned. The social worker then told her she would call her right back.

I decided to find out if we could get an earlier appointment for our girls' medical appointment. This is the same place that we currently were scheduled for next Tuesday. IAN staff has not been forthcoming about a lot of things, so I wanted to find out if we really needed to wait for the girls' passports to get their required physicals for the Embassy papers to be submitted. The first receptionist with whom I spoke told me all we needed were their birth certificates, but to check in the medical office. I then learned that for US adoptions, passports were necessary for the physical. I went on to ask if we could get an appointment on Friday if I had the passports. She said that they may be able to get us in, but if not, then we could make an appointment for Monday. She said the report could be ready the same day.

Now that we were armed with this knowledge, we realized that submission to Embassy could be done sooner than we had been led to believe. Andrea dialed the IAN office again and there was no answer. This is when we realized that it might be most productive to actually go to the office and confront them in person.

The unfortunate part is that it was 4:30 p.m. and we did not know the address or how to get there. We did, however, have a driver that was willing to help us find this unknown address. We put on our "spy gear" as James called it and started our investigation. I remembered it was in the Bole district and that there were several manikins lined up along the street of the office (something I had not seen anywhere else in the city). Andrea remembered a French restaurant, and Frank remembered miniature Eiffel Towers out front. Tehut was asking a couple taxi drivers if they knew of a French restaurant in the Bole district, but when Frank mentioned the Eiffel Towers, I yelled out, "Paris Cafe!" and began using my hands to describe the Eiffel Tower. They gave Tehut a general idea of where they had seen such a place, and we were on our way.

We tried to call the Afro Land Lodge to ask Michael to look it up on the Internet. There was no answer. We all started looking through our iPhone emails to see if we could locate an old email with the contact list. Frank had success, only it gave a general area, not an exact address. We were getting closer. As soon as we entered the neighborhood and saw the manikins lined up along the street, I looked up and shouted, "The DHL building, I remember that building!" Tehut drove closer, and we all got excited when we saw the Paris Cafe. We all exclaimed at the same time, "That's it, that's the building!" Tehut turned on to the street and we all shuffled out and ran into the building.

I said, "Let's split up between the elevator and the stairs so we don't miss them in case they're leaving." Andrea ran toward the stairs, so I went to the elevator to press the button just as a man informed me that the elevator was closed for the day. I grabbed James' hand and we all went up the stairs to the fourth floor. The door to the office was open. We had not missed the staff. We walked into the office, and the staff was all there. Andrea sat down to talk to the woman who had lied, and withheld information several times. Upon further interrogation, she learned that they could not submit their paperwork to Embassy tomorrow because the court documents were inaccurate. Apparently, the father had been listed as deceased, although he was said to be unknown by the mother. She said the only way to change the documents is if the birth mother went to the court to set the record straight. Again, all information that had been known for a while and withheld. The birth mother lived in Gambia, a plane trip away.

After several excuses and changing stories, the director got on the phone and booked a flight. The birth mom was located and would be in Addis Ababa tomorrow. We suggested that the paperwork be submitted anyway and let the rest run its course as to at least get the ball rolling. At that point I explained what I had learned at IOM and demanded that we pick up the passports on Friday and drive to IOM to make an appointment. Then we could submit to Embassy for the visas on Wednesday of next week rather than wait until the following. They agreed this could all be done. I expect them to follow through with this agreement. After all, we did pay them thousands of dollars to do their job. We paid twice since we have twins. Referral cost total, $18,000. The looks on their faces, priceless.

7/2/13

Bekele arrived at 8:00 a.m. to drive us to IOM for the girls' physicals. James stayed at the hotel with Andrea's family and watched Star Wars: Episode 3 Revenge of the Sith. Nigist met us at the entrance of IOM at 8:30. IOM has a security check as you walk in. Then they give a visitors pass to each adult. Nigist then showed her credentials, and we walked into the main building, up to the second floor. There were about twenty people sitting in chairs that lined the hallway. Nigist guided us into the nurse's station, but she was told to go pay at reception first. We went back out into the hallway and waited. The girls' breakfast time is at 9:00 a.m., so I fed them a banana while it was possible. Everyone is staring at us. About 15 minutes later, Nigist came back and told us we had to wait for the nurse to come upstairs. We waited for 10 minutes and the nurse came up and escorted us in to have the girls weighed and measured.

After he was done measuring and weighing them, my husband sat down while administrative paperwork was being completed. He then checked it and signed as the father. Mike then gave the administrator the immunization records to enter into the database for the medical report. Next, we were asked to wait in the hallway to see the doctor for their exam. By this time, the place was nearly full with people waiting to be seen.

Zoey has a new tooth coming in and had been cranky the past three days. She started being fussy. So I gave her some homeopathic pills. About 15 minutes later, we went into the doctor's office and she continued her fussiness, so again I gave her two more pills. She was fine after that. The doctor asked a few questions about their development. We told her that since we took custody, they were now rolling over and Zoey was pulling herself up and starting to crawl. The doctor suggested that they were a little developmentally delayed, and Mike explained that they did not get floor time in the orphanage to practice their skills (they would cry in their crib and get placed on the floor in a Bumbo) and they were now catching up.

The girls were then undressed and examined. The doctor listened to their chest and heart. Zoey grabbed the stethoscope and showed the doctor her super strong grip. She was impressed by her strength.

Once the exam was complete, she euphemistically stated that the girls were well nourished—code for chunky. There were no concerns and the girls passed. This was great news. The medical report would be completed by the afternoon and ready to submit to the U.S. Embassy. Nigist said she would pick up the hard copy tomorrow morning since she had to bring another family then.

Yay! This means all our work was done, and we could have our case submitted to Embassy tomorrow. The next step is to be accepted for the issuance of the girls' visas to enter the U.S.A.

When we returned to the Afro Land Lodge, I took pictures and sent my family an email: "Guess what? My sister and I passed our physicals yesterday so we were able to request travel visas from the U.S. Embassy today. We are excited! See you as soon as we can!" Ellie and Zoey

7/3/13

Today we (Andrea's family, James and I) went to Entoto Beth Artisan, which is an organization that trains women who are HIV+ to do artisan work; paying them a fair wage for their work. They create handcrafted jewelry using recycled materials such as bullet castings from past wars. Currently they are training women how to weave baskets. The baskets will go on sale in about two months. They are beautiful. We got to visit the two workshops. There were 25 women, 8 making baskets, and the others beading jewelry. We bought several lovely pieces of jewelry in the on-site store.

Next, Tehut drove us to the Africa Leprosy, Tuberculosis, and Rehabilitation Training (ALERT) Centre. (They were open this time.) Several textiles are made and sold at this facility. I purchased some pillow covers that are embroidered with traditional symbols.

The next stop was the IAN office to check on our status. We walked into the office and the birth mother for Andrea's son was there waiting to be taken to the airport for her flight back home. Andrea then learned that she had missed her email that morning, and that they had been cleared by the U.S. Embassy to get their son's visa on Friday.

Although the unexpected meeting with the birth mom was a bit awkward—we had not told the agency we were stopping by, so it was not planned—the news was very good. I then checked with the social worker to make sure the twins' files were being submitted. The files were bundled on his desk. He was scheduled to take them at 2:00 p.m. Excellent!

We went out for Ethiopian food later to celebrate. Very yummy!

7/4/13

Fourth of July in Ethiopia isn't the same as being in the United States, but we celebrated anyway. Permera's family and ours went up to the roof top of the Afro Lodge in the evening. We took some American style food and had a picnic with a view. We ate potato salad, corn on the cob, and watermelon. We sang the National Anthem and lit sparklers. Having been pining for home we felt a bit of relief and comfort in our nostalgic celebration.

7/5/13

Family checklist for our Embassy trip: I-864 (W), Visa 37 confirmation email, Embassy clearance and appointment confirmation emails, Original I-171H plus one copy, Passports

From: Barbara Robertson Horner

Sent: Friday, July 05, 2013, 8:38 a.m.

To: Addis, Adoption

Subject: Robertson Horner case

Good Morning Taye,

Our social worker at IAN informed us that he submitted our twins, Marta and Merma's Embassy paperwork on Wednesday. Please confirm that this is true.

We, Michael, Barbara, and our 5-year-old son, James, have been in Addis Ababa since June 1st. We are eager to get home to California so that we can give our girls the best care possible. Michael's work is pressing for his return, and it would be much easier for me to care for and travel with the three kids if Michael is here to help.

We would appreciate it if our case could be approved as soon as possible.

Thank you for your attention to our case.

Sincerely,

Barbara and Michael Robertson Horner

Sent: Friday, July 5, 2013

To: Barbara Robertson Horner

Dear Robertsonhorner Family:

Congratulations! Your adoption cases have been submitted to the U.S. Embassy in Addis Ababa, Ethiopia. Your authorized agent, International Adoption Net, submitted the case to us on July 5, 2013. The name of the beneficiary in your case is:

Robertsonhorner, Merma and Marta Michael (ADD2011689039).

The case submitted contained the following documents:

- An adoption decree from the Federal First Instance Court

- Approval letters from the Ministry of Women, Children and Youth Affairs

- The child's birth certificate and Ethiopian passport

- Form I-600, Petition to Classify Orphan as an Immediate Relative.

- Visa processing fee (please note that our visa fee decreased from $404 to $230 on April 13, 2012. You paid the new, lower fee).

- Other supporting documentation

Now that we have received the Form I-600 petition and accompanying documentation, we will begin our required orphan status determination (Form I-604, Determination on Child for Adoption) —the process to investigate whether the child meets the definition of an orphan under U.S. immigration law. We start these investigations in the order in which the cases were received, but completion of the Form I-604 determination depends on the unique circumstances of each case and can take up to several weeks or months. During this time, we may request additional information or documentation from you for cases with insufficient or deficient supporting evidence to determine orphan status.

In many cases the consular officer requests an interview with the child's Ethiopian birth parent(s) or guardian, or an individual or police officer who found or was involved in the case of an abandoned child, to resolve questions, errors or discrepancies discovered in the case file. These interviews are often necessary to make a determination regarding the child's orphan status. Birth relative and other interviews are often an integral part of the Form I-604 determination and a normal part of the process.

The U.S. Embassy maintains a very tight schedule for birth relative and child finder interviews. These interviews are scheduled weeks and sometimes months in advance and you and your appointed adoption service provider will be notified well in advance of the date and time of these interviews. Please help us process your case quickly by ensuring that your adoption service agent arrives promptly at the appointed date and time for these interviews. Rescheduling these interviews can prolong the processing of your case by weeks or months.

We recognize that the case review process is an anxious time for adoptive parents. The consular officer reviews each case carefully. You will receive an update by email whenever the status of your case changes. If you have not received an email, it means that your case is still pending the completion of the Form I-604 determination and the overall status remains unchanged. We will try to answer all your questions and concerns as quickly as possible, but we are often unable to answer specific inquiries until after we have completed our processing. Please be aware that some cases take longer to process than others for a variety of reasons, but often because requested documentation is submitted late or interviews with birth relatives and child finders must be rescheduled. Please ensure that your adoption service provider complies with our requests as quickly as possible so that we can provide you the best possible service.

After we have reviewed all the submitted and requested documentation and conducted all the necessary interviews and field investigations, we will determine if your case is clearly approvable. If your Form I-600 petition is clearly approvable, we will advise you that your petition has been approved and work with you to schedule an appointment date for the consular interview. If there are questions regarding your child's orphan status or the information is insufficient to make a determination, U.S. federal regulation requires us to forward the case as "not clearly approvable" to the USCIS Field Office in Nairobi, Kenya, for further processing. Due to the high number of children who have been found abandoned, we should note that it has not always been possible to establish that the petition beneficiaries in these circumstances is clearly an orphan. If your case is determined to be "not clearly approvable," then we will notify you when the case is physically forwarded to USCIS Nairobi, and provide contact information for further questions.

Upon receipt of a petition identified as "not clearly approvable," the USCIS Nairobi Field Office notifies the parent(s) that the case has been received and takes other appropriate steps to complete the case and will be in touch with the petitioners directly. For more details on the USCIS process, please visit USCIS' Ethiopia Q&A page.

We recognize that the adoption process is long and involves many steps. We will do everything we can to ensure that your case is processed as expeditiously as possible.

With best regards,

Steve Remitz

Chief of the Consular Section

7/8/13

From: Barbara Robertson Horner

Sent: Monday, July 08, 2013, 1:15 a.m.

To: Suri Laney

Subject: Still in Ethiopia

Good morning Suri. Hope all is well! As you know I was expecting to be back home by now; however, due to some issues with our team we have run into delays. The Embassy has our paperwork and is reviewing it. They do not give us a specific timeline so I am not sure when we will be cleared, hopefully soon! I requested family leave through FMLA until this last Friday 7/5/13. So it has now expired. May I now use vacation time as I have no other recourse until we get back home. We hope to see you soon. I will keep you updated as we get more info from the Embassy.

Thanks so much,

Michael

To: Michael Robertson Horner

Sent: Monday, July 8, 2013, 10:30 p.m.

Subject: RE: Still in Ethiopia

Hi Michael,

I'm sorry to hear you are having to play the 'waiting game', but hopefully it will all be a distant memory soon and you'll be home with your wonderful family.

Please do not worry at all about your time off. You are entitled to 12 weeks protected FMLA leave to bond/care for newly adopted children, so at this point we will simply extend your leave end date. The only thing you need to let me know is how to pay you. Have you been using SDI to supplement the 23 hrs/pp we've been sending? If so, that will be stopping at the end of 6 weeks leave. So you have three options: 1. continue to use 23 hrs/pp without supplementation from SDI, or 2. go back to full pay from Stanford and use your vacation balance to do so. I checked with Reba, your July 10th check is the first one to use any vacation time, previously you were using sick time, which is now depleted. So you still have vacation hours on the books to cover approximately 8 weeks of full time pay if you wish, or 3. Let us know how many vacation hours you would like to use if there is a different amount you prefer.

Additionally, if for some goofy reason this were to take longer than you have vacation time/FMLA for, you simply need to request personal leave in an email to Carl and Darren. I do not anticipate any concerns on their part, we are all supportive and excited for this venture and will help any way we can.

Take care,

Suri

To: Barbara Robertson Horner

Sent: Jul 8, 2013, at 11:45 a.m.

Thank you for your email. This is to confirm that we have received your cases on July 5, 2013. Your cases are in queue to be reviewed as we process the cases in the order we receive them. We will contact you when the status of the case is changed.

Regards

Adoption Unit

From: Barbara Robertson Horner

Sent: Monday, July 08, 2013, 12:01 p.m.

To: Addis, Adoption

Subject: Re: Robertson Horner case

Dear Taye,

Thank you very much for the contact. We look forward to working with you. Do you have a preliminary timeline for us? I need to communicate with my employer because they are pressing for my return.

Sincerely,

Michael Robertson Horner

From: Barbara Robertson Horner

Sent July 8, 2003

To: Andrea

Hi Andrea,

Afro Land wants us to move out tomorrow. The manager booked the whole hotel for a big party. He offered us the owner's apartment next door. Apparently there is a six-year-old girl living there as well. Very strange. We will have to look at it in the morning to see if it works for us. I'm perplexed. Do you know of any other place?

Cheers,

Barbara and Fam

7/9/13

To: Barbara Robertson Horner

Sent: Jul 9, 2013, at 11:00 a.m.

Thank you for your email. Unfortunately we don't have a timeline to provide you. That is why we do not recommend the families to travel to Ethiopia before the case is cleared for a visa interview. We will contact you whenever the status of your cases changes.

Regards

Adoption Unit

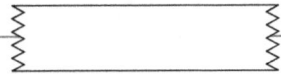

From: Barbara Robertson Horner

Sent: Tuesday, July 09, 2013, 11:38 a.m.

To: Addis, Adoption

Subject: Re: Robertson Horner case

Thank you for the correspondence. I do understand that a speculative or definitive timeline cannot be provided at this time. We chose to stay in Addis for the benefit of our daughters; even a short time in an orphanage is too long for any child. Since bringing them into our family they have blossomed and grown. I look forward to getting them into the stability of our home in the states; there they will truly thrive. I will do my best to stave off my employer so that I can continue to directly support my family through this process. Any help that you can provide in making this happen will be of great support to my family and much celebrated.

Best regards,

Michael

To: Barbara Robertson Horner

Sent: Friday, July 05, 2013

Barbara,

Omg - seriously??!? I'm so sorry! You should check out Yeka House. The rooms are not as nice but the common spaces are great and I really think that the community there will make up for more cramped living space.

I'll research a few more in the morning but that's all I have right now.

How on earth could they ask that of you??!? That's crazy! How long would you have to move out for?

Permera has somehow miraculously changed to eastern time just by arriving so while getting him (and us)into a routine in our house will take a few more days, at least he's sleeping.

Our luggage was found and will allegedly get here tomorrow (Tuesday) night. Small miracles!

Andrea

Tues, Jul 9, 2013

From: Barbara Robertson Horner

To: Andrea

Hi Andrea,

Glad your luggage was found. Permera must be happy in his new home. No roosters or prayer to wake him.

We will move into the apartment and see how it goes. It has its own kitchen, but no TV. The manager said he will bring over a TV and attempt to hook up the cable. It's actually attached, not combined with the owner's apt.

You missed a major argument outside the hotel that was quelled by a mob of about 45. Some guys had sticks and another had a tire iron. The manager had to call the police.

Wish we were home. I wonder if Taye got in trouble for expediting your case, so they won't hurry ours.

Take care,

Barbara

7/9/2013

We moved out of Afro Lodge and paid our total from 6/8/13 – 7/9/13 and moved to the apartment. We will miss our sweet guest house with daily breakfast. Sad to have to leave. Not sure we like the place they put us.

To: Barbara Robertson Horner

Sent: July 9, 2013

RE: International Adoption Net 7-10-2013

Dear Mr. and Mrs. Robertson Horner:

REF: Case No. ADD2011689039 Merma Michael Robertson Horner and ADD2013191001 Marta Michael Robertson Horner

We would like to inform you the consular section completed screening for your Form I-600 petition. We will now begin the review of orphan status for the I-604, Determination on Child for Adoption. As part of this process, we may request additional information or documents as it becomes necessary throughout the I-604 process. You will receive notice when processing is complete.

Sincerely,

Adoption Unit

U.S. Embassy Addis Ababa

To: Barbara Robertson Horner

Sent: Wednesday, July 10, 2013, 5:20 p.m.

Subject: RE: Robertson Horner case

Dear Robertson Horner family,

Do you or your agency have any evidence to show that a search was conducted for the birth mother after she disappeared? Based on what's in the file, it appears that a newspaper advertisement was run in the

Addis Zemen newspaper, but since the woman was from Gambella it's hard to know if anyone actually looked for her there. We require evidence that she has actually disappeared in order to document the children as orphans.

Your agency can bring the evidence of a police search to the embassy at any time during our business hours.

Thanks,

Taye Davis

Vice Consul, Adoptions

US Embassy Addis Ababa

To: Barbara Robertson Horner

Sent: Thursday, July 11, 2013

Barbara,

Holy crap - sticks and a tire iron??!?!?!? Oh dear lord! How is the apt working out? You doing ok? Did they help with the move? I hope you're at least able to settle in a bit. I'm so sorry—will they have you move back into your current place next week?

I'm not sure what's with Taye and you guys... his emails are so much more curt than they were with us, it seems really strange. I get that with an abandonment vs a relinquishment it is a different process that they go through but I think it's really weird that they wouldn't give you a timeframe at all. Permera explored our backyard today - we had a taste of landscaping stones and sticks and we loved it!

How is James doing? Squeeze those sweet girls for us!

Andrea

From: Barbara Robertson Horner

Sent: Friday, Jul 12, 2013

Hi Andrea,

We moved to the Panorama Hotel. The apt. had no internet, phone, or T.V., the shower was a drip and the place reminded me of a dump I lived in for two months when I was 18. For $103 per night, we have a lovely hotel room with a view of mountains and no roosters. There is a restaurant and bar, a gym, and a spa. I think I will get a massage today. The U.S. Embassy requested evidence from Gambella that there was a search done to locate the birth mom. IAN requested and received the report yesterday and gave it to the Embassy (so they say). Once this is checked out, we should get our Embassy appointment.

Fingers crossed! The wireless is not working here since last night, but the lobby internet is, so I need to use it at present.

Funny how we left Addis View because there was no water and we had water issues at Afro Land. We left Afro Land because we had no Internet, and now we have Internet issues at the Panorama.

Hugs to Premera.

Take care,

Barbara

From: Barbara Robertson Horner

Sent: July 12, 2013

Dear Taye,

Our agency said they gave you the evidence yesterday. Please confirm this occurred. Was it what was needed to complete the approval of the adoption?

Thanks for your reply,

Barbara and Michael

———————————————————————————————

To Barbara Robertson Horner

Sent: Friday, July 12, 2013

Barbara,

View of the mountains??!? Gym and spa??!? I love that! I'm so sorry you had to move but glad it's working out. How's James handling leaving his friends? If the Internet is back up tomorrow, want to FaceTime?

I love that IAN had what Embassy wanted on hand. I'm sure that'll move things along for a soooooon Embassy. I can feel it now!!!

Oh and our St. George mugs all made it safely here - we were so surprised that none broke! It'll be time for you to pack (again) soon and then a much smoother travel than we had. I cannot wait to hear the good news!

Tell me about your massage so I can live vicariously through you!

Andrea

7/12/13

James is making friends with the staff again. He has a new lady friend named Sitota. He hangs out and sits on her lap and helps her with registration. Sort of, haha. Bought a large, beautiful painting of an Ethiopian woman in a lovely ceremonial dress.

Received this info today:

IAN Family Itinerary cont. Embassy Day pick us up from our hotel. M/W 8:00 a.m. , T/Th 12 noon have I-864 (W) IAN coffee ceremony at IAN Care Center.

We will receive birth certificate, child's visa adoption decree, and child's passport with visa sticker attached.

Upon leaving we received a sealed envelope that we were told not to open. This envelope will be given to customs (Documents pertaining to child's visa.)

Upon arrival in US, the immigration officer will request the sealed envelope. We can request the medical form from the officer- we must request the immunization record from IAN staff at the beginning of our trip.

7/13/13

We moved to a new hotel, Panorama Hotel on Thursday. The WiFi stopped working on Friday. We hope it is fixed today. The hotel is great otherwise. There is a gym and spa. I got a massage :-). We went on a tour Saturday. It was very nice. No good news yet from Embassy.

From: Barbara Robertson Horner

Sent: Monday July 15, 2013, 10:49 a.m.

Andrea

Still no WiFi-

Barbara

_____

From: Barbara Robertson Horner

Sent: Monday, July 15, 2013

Andrea,

We cleared!!! Awaiting our Embassy appt. date.

Barbara

To: Barbara Robertson Horner

Sent: Monday, July 15, 2013

Barbara,

Omg - that's great! Do you have enough Internet to book the tix or do you need me to help?

Andrea

_____

From: Barbara Robertson Horner

Sent: Tuesday, July 16, 2013

Andrea

I might need help. There was no Internet in lobby last night, but there is today. I will try today and let you know. Thanks

Barbara

To: Barbara Robertson Horner

Tuesday, July 16, 2013, 2:51 p.m.

Barbara,

Just let me know - I'm here at the ready!

Andrea

————————————————————————————

From: Barbara Robertson Horner

Sent: Tuesday, Jul 16, 2013, at 11:11 a.m.

Andrea,

I have no Internet or WiFi. I am at an INTERNET OUTLET. I can't get any tickets for under $6000 for us. I had tickets for under $5000 this morning and lost access. We get the girls' visas Thursday morning. We had the meeting today. Please help.

Barbara

————————————————————————————

To: Barbara Robertson Horner

Sent: Tuesday, July 16, 2013, at 11:14 a.m.

Barbara,

You want to leave Thursday or as soon as possible I assume?

Andrea

To: Barbara Robertson Horner

Sent: Tuesday, July 16, 2013, 6:23 p.m.

Barbara

I've got flights to San Francisco for $888 each on Friday.

Andrea

————————————————————

From: Barbara Robertson Horner

Sent: Tuesday, July 16, 2013, at 11:37 a.m.

Andrea,

You have my info and visa, so go ahead and book. I have to go now. My ride back to the hotel is here. I will try to connect later or tomorrow for sure. Thanks.

Barbara

————————————————————

To: Barbara Robertson Horner

Sent: Tuesday, July 16, 2013, at 11:39 a.m.

Oh dear - are you willing to go another three hundred a person for San Francisco?

Andrea

To: Barbara Robertson Horner

Sent: Tuesday, July 16, 2013

Barbara,

It's more than you wanted but it was this or a fourth stop with an overnight at JFK. I'm calling to work on your seats now.

Andrea

United Confirmation Number HW3ZY8

Purchase Summary

2 Infants (under age 2 at time of travel) $176.00

2 Adults (age 18 to 64) $3,726.00

1 Child $1,863.00

Additional Taxes/Fees $377.10

Total $6,142.10

Fri., Jul. 19, 2013, Addis Ababa ET (ADD) to Sacramento, CA (SMF)

Depart: 10:50 p.m.

Fri., Jul. 19, 2013, Addis Ababa ET (ADD)

Arrive: 6:55 a.m. +1 Day

Sat., Jul. 20, 2013, Frankfurt, Germany(FRA)

Flight Time: 9 hr 5 mn

Distance: 319 miles

Flight: UA9137

Operated by Lufthansa.

Aircraft: Airbus A330-300

Fare Class: United Economy (V)

Meal: Snack or Brunch

No Special Meal Offered.

1 Stop. Time on the ground in Khartoum, Sudan (KRT) is 1 hour 15 minutes.

Change Planes. Connect time in Frankfurt, Germany (FRA) is 2 hours 45 minutes.

Depart: 9:40 a.m.

Sat., Jul. 20, 2013, Frankfurt, Germany(FRA)

Arrive: 12:30 p.m.

Sat., Jul. 20, 2013, Washington, DC (IAD -Dulles)

Flight Time: 8 hr 50mn

Distance: 4,081 miles

Flight: UA8832

Operated by Lufthansa Aircraft: Airbus A330-300

Fare Class: Economy (V)

Meal: Snack or Brunch

No Special Meal Offered

Change Planes. Connect time in Washington, DC (IAD -Dulles) is 5 hours 3 minutes.

Depart: 5:33 p.m.

Sat., Jul. 20, 2013, Washington, DC (IAD -Dulles)

Arrive: 8:16 p.m.

Sat., Jul. 20,2013, Sacramento, CA (SMF)

Flight Time: 5 hr 43 mn

Travel Time: 31 hr 26 mn

Distance: 2,358 miles

Total Distance: 9,758 miles

Flight: UA291

Aircraft: Airbus A320

Fare Class: United Economy (M)

Meal: Food for Purchase -No Special Meal Offered.

rom: Barbara Robertson Horner

Sent: Wednesday, July 17, 2013

Andrea,

Thanks. You are a superstar! Did you request meals? Do I need to call to do this?

Barbara

7/17/13

Today we will be picked up by Getachew to partake in the coffee ritual at the orphanage (IAN Care Center). It was a sweet ritual. We had some fruit and cake with the coffee. It was a nice touch to say goodbye more formally to the place our girls had been living for six months of their life between their birth mom and their new forever family.

Left Addis at 10:15 p.m. July 19 to Khartoum July 20 (stop) to Frankfurt at 6:55 a.m. –9:40 a.m. (layover) to Washington DC at 12:30 p.m.– 17:33 p.m. (layover) to Sacramento July 20, 8:16 p.m.

Looking back on our two months in Ethiopia, I'm filled with a unique blend of gratitude, nostalgia, and amazement at all our family experienced together. Those weeks spent living in Addis Ababa—navigating daily life with our five-year-old son James while finalizing the adoption of our twin daughters— truly shaped us into a family of five in ways we never could have imagined.

There had certainly been moments of inconvenience: the constant construction, bumpy roads, lack of sidewalks, and the unpredictable traffic that made each outing an adventure. I know I often found myself longing for the simple comforts and smoother routines of life in California.

Yet in reflecting on our time living here, it's not the difficulties that linger in my heart. More than anything, I cherish the memories of Ethiopia's lush green hills, the rich history, and, most of all, the incredible people we met along the way. The warmth and openness of the locals, the friends we made over shared meals and coffee, and the kindness extended to our growing family left an impression that time cannot fade.

As we prepared to return home, I felt deeply grateful for this extraordinary chapter. Our perspectives broadened, our hearts grew, and our family became complete. Ethiopia will always be part of our story and as we return to California, we will treasure the warmth, joy, and special connections we made.

Section 6

Coming to America

As we touched down on American soil, we began more than just a journey home—we started a new chapter as a family. Blending cultures from Ethiopia, Vietnam, and our new life in the United States, we are now an American family, united in love and ready to celebrate every part of our interwoven story together.

Chapter 16

The moment our plane landed in Washington DC, our girls became official U.S. citizens, and in that moment, we truly became an official family. Interestingly, even though my daughters were Black, they were not African Americans since they immigrated in 2013. Unlike many Blacks in America, they know where they originated in Africa—in Ethiopia. So that makes them Ethiopian Americans. Although labels are not something I care for, they now live in a country known for categorizing people. Truth be told, we are all children of God. But now the labeling, identities, and racist constructs begin.

Arriving in Sacramento was such a relief. We had made it home—our hearts full and our arms filled with family. As we entered the baggage claim, my friend Hue was awaiting us with open arms to welcome our new family home. Home! Home felt good—familiar, comfortable, and just what we needed after so long away and an exhausting plane ride. It was evening and we were completely spent, so celebrations and excursions would have to wait. We were sleepy and jet lagged—going home, getting some rest, and helping the girls settle in took precedence over everything and anyone. All that really mattered was finally having the comfort of our own space, a place to finally unwind together and simply be a family.

Over the next two weeks, we soaked up every moment at home, showing the girls their playroom and shared bedroom, playing dress-up, picking out new clothes, and introducing them to all sorts of foods and our curious cats. James loved being their tour guide, giving the girls the lowdown on every corner of the house and helping them discover their new world. Every day brought small joys and discoveries—laughter echoing through the house, tiny hands reaching for new toys, the simple happiness of finally playing "family" for real. After twenty years of hoping and wishing, having my family complete and sharing these moments together filled our home with a happiness I'd waited a lifetime to feel.

Our first big event for the twins was a baby shower thrown by my coworkers, conveniently right in our own home. It was wonderful to see everyone gathered together, meeting the girls for the first time and taking turns holding them. At 11 months old, the twins were crawling constantly and full of energy, happily soaking up all the attention. I felt so accepted and cared for by my coworkers. The baby shower was truly a warm welcome for our new, complete family. It was so good to be home.

Two months in Ethiopia—living out of hotels, making court visits, going to doctor's appointments, and navigating a completely foreign society, all while slowly finding our rhythm as a family. I have no regrets about staying in Ethiopia even though it was a challenging experience. It was a great growth period and gave us a wonderful understanding of the girls' culture that we could share with them moving forward. I think the hardest part of adopting children of another culture and race is not having that lived experience to share with them. We are White and living in the United

States. We have privileges afforded to us that they will only experience through association. Though we will never fully understand the experience of growing up Black and Asian in this country, we can expose our children to their culture through education and programs that support them. I am truly grateful to have my life enriched in this way. So worth the road ahead, I wouldn't have it any different. Our life will be richer for it.

Even though we had taken classes through the adoption agency, the best way for me to learn was through my own lived experience as a White mom with beautiful kids of color. I knew our family might draw some attention when we were out and about—I just hoped it wouldn't happen as often as it does.

Sometimes a simple trip to the grocery store included lingering glances or off-color remarks and questions from strangers. There were times when people would ask me things like, "Are you their nanny?" or "Are you babysitting?" I can't recall ever asking anyone these questions myself—at least not unless I really knew them well. I understand that as humans, we are naturally curious, but sometimes that curiosity can cross a line and become intrusive, or even a little hurtful.

Being a mom of twins brings its own set of funny moments, too. I can't count the number of times people would stop me and ask, "Are they twins?" or "Are they identical?" And when someone has twins in their family, it's a must to let other twin parents know. "I have twins," or "My siblings are twins." Another common comment, "You have your hands full." All questions my other twin mom friends can relate to.

Having children opens up a world of communication with strangers that I would have otherwise never experienced. Whether the encounters are awkward, kind, or simply funny, they're all part of this unique journey of motherhood. Each time I am reminded that most people are just trying to find connection, even if their approach might be a little clumsy.

Honestly, I kind of expected comments from White people when I adopted my Ethiopian twins—but I wasn't ready for just how much attention I'd get all around. I'd get remarks from Black folks too, like "You are such an angel to adopt these babies," or "Do you need someone to do their hair?" I get that a lot of people mean well, though it's not always the case.

Truth—I felt like I was the one who was blessed to have these kids. And as for hair? I had zero experience with type 4c hair (the most tightly coiled, curly hair). I spent a lot of late nights googling just how to get it right.

Some people looked at us with genuine warmth or curiosity, while others had a more questioning or even skeptical look—almost as if they were silently asking what a White woman was doing with Black kids? I would either get smiles or head shakes. I learned quickly that what mattered most was that these were my babies and what others thought did not define my family. I developed a bubble where I kept my focus on my children. I didn't want to know if people were staring. It was like mama bear protecting her cubs.

School would be starting soon, and we needed to put our girls into childcare. I assumed that we would enroll them in the Montessori childcare where James went to preschool, but they told us there were no openings. So, we looked onto care.com to find a nanny. We had three we were interested in interviewing. After careful consideration we decided on a woman in her early thirties. She seemed more natural with them. Still, I really wished I could be a stay-at-home mom. The cost of childcare did make me wonder why I even bothered to work when half of my paycheck was paying for childcare. But it was a relief to have this figured out.

My niece Britney (who had lived with us in Sacramento) was getting married in Portland, Oregon, at the end of August and I would have to miss the second day of school in order to attend. I really wanted to go, as it was an opportunity to introduce the girls to our large extended family in Portland. Where we lived, we didn't have family nearby. The timing was tough—my need to be with family happened right at the beginning of the school year, which is one of the most demanding times for any teacher. As difficult as it was to risk adjustment issues with my students, I knew my children had to come first. This was just one of many hard choices I'd face as I tried to balance teaching with raising a family.

Before long, we found ourselves in Portland, introducing the twins to their new family. The joy was unmistakable—everyone was celebrating, connecting, and just so happy to be together. It was so worth it to put my family before my job for this. Still, as the visit ended, I knew it was time to head back and meet my new class—even if a big part of me would've rather stayed home with my beautiful kids.

This school year I had opted to teach a new grade at our school, Transitional Kindergarten. Since the age cut off for kindergarten was now October 1, all students turning five between October 1 and December 31 would be in my class. It was a very active school day with eighteen four-year-olds. Although, I wouldn't have work to take home, and I could leave at the end of the day instead of having to stay late to plan lessons. Lesson planning at this age level was quicker and easier than teaching fifth grade. It was a perfect fit for having twin babies to go home to. If I could leave by three, I could lower my commute from 60 to 35 minutes.

When I would come home, the girls would look at me as if to ask where I had been. And yet, they also seemed to be wondering with curious eyes who I was. It was heartbreaking and I really was pining to be a stay-at-home mom. I thought about taking the next year off, but I didn't have enough savings to afford that option. So I continued to think of ways to make money from home.

It was December when I was invited to a free three-day event called The Millionaire Mind Intensive (MMI). I went with my friend Hue. We were still trying to get me successful in selling from a Multi-level marketing(MLM) company. I met someone at the event who signed up to sell in the company. That got me excited. The MMI really got me hyped up. I was so thrilled with the sales pitch for classes that I signed up for the package deal: Life Directions, Wizard Training, and Train the Trainer. Peak Potentials had bought the company from its original owner T. Harv Eker. I had an education fund that my father had set up for me. I was able to access it to pay for the classes. I was on my way to figure out how to leave education and start a home business—or so I thought. But before I could pursue that next step to live my dream of being a stay-at-home mom with a flexible home business, I needed to press pause and keep a promise I had made to myself years earlier.

Chapter 17

Back when I adopted James, I had made a promise that I would take him to Vietnam every five years. It was 2014 and time to follow up on my promise. I started planning for our trip and decided Spring Break would be an ideal time. This would be in April and just before James' 6th birthday. I knew this would be quite the undertaking for us with one-year-old twins in tow, yet I was determined to keep my promise. Luckily, my sister Bonnie offered to go along and help with the kids. This seemed like a perfect solution to a daunting travel task.

Making this trip happen for all six of us meant careful planning and organization. I had to get passports in order. Flights needed to be booked. Then there was the hotel booking for all six of us. I needed a tentative itinerary of things we would like to do. Then I needed to read up on and understand the rules and regulations for getting there. I had to set up our visas. According to the rules, we could get our visas when we entered Vietnam in the airport.

Next, I would pack all the necessary kid stuff without over-packing. Deciding to bring strollers and car seats was a bit of a dilemma. Honestly, I grew up in an era before seatbelts, car seats, or helmets were the norm, so I don't always feel pressed to go overboard with safety gear the way younger parents might. Chalk it up to being part of Generation X—we just learned to roll with life's bumps and bruises.

It was finally time for our trip and Bonnie had flown down to Sacramento to go with us. We flew from Sacramento to LAX to connect to our international flight, which included a short layover in Seoul, Korea before flying on to Ho Chi Minh City, Vietnam. We went to the airline desk to check in and were asked for our visas. I told them we were planning to get our visas in Vietnam. The airline attendant said, "I'm sorry, you can't get on this flight because it stops in Korea, and you need a visa to stop in Korea."

At first, I just stood there, my mouth agape, in total shock and denial. I looked at the attendant and said, "NO!" I was not about to accept this. After all I had done to set up this trip, I was not about to cry and go home. I began pleading that there had to be a way to correct this problem. My sister called it going into "Barbara mode"—when every ounce of my strength and perseverance comes alive, and I become unstoppable in pursuit of my goals. I told them my story: the promise, James' birthday, in charge of planning for all 6, non-refundable tickets and hotel, my sister flew down from Portland…

After much explaining about how important this trip was to my adopted son, I implored them to help me find a solution. The attendant felt compassion for me and said that I could buy visas last minute through an online site, but it would be more money—and there might not be enough time to get them before the flight had to leave. I said I was willing to take that chance and was allowed to go behind the counter into the Airline office to use their computer.

I told my family to go through security and head to the gate. I said I would make this right and meet them as soon as I got the visas. I went into the office, got onto the computer, and got to work. This was probably the most stressful nonphysical experience of my life and I was determined to stay hyper focused until my mission was accomplished.

Once I got the visas, I ran to security and the airline got me up to the front quickly. I then ran to the gate and made it just five minutes before boarding closed. I could feel the cortisol shooting through my body, followed by a sharp dopamine rush. I was exhausted both mentally and physically, yet relieved. The tension released in my shoulders and I let out a deep sigh. My muscles were relaxing, and I was ready to sit down and order a cocktail.

Thank the powers that be, we made it. If God gives us only what we can handle, He must think I'm pretty badass. We were on our way to Vietnam, a miracle at best.

When we arrived in Korea, our visas had already been sent to the customs and immigration office, and we had them complete and in our hands within 45 minutes. Whew! Another hit of dopamine for me. We were able to board our flight to Vietnam.

While taking the taxi to our hotel, I noticed that Vietnam had developed in the five years since we had last been. There were many more traffic lights. A good improvement from the craziness we experienced before, though still very congested. James couldn't stop laughing at the sight of entire families—sometimes four people at once—all piled onto a single motorbike zipping through the streets of Ho Chi Minh City, a.k.a. Saigon. It was such a wild, unexpected sight for him, and his laughter was infectious as he pointed out each new motorbike family, completely amazed and delighted by the organized chaos of it all.

Our hotel turned out to be a wonderful retreat in itself. We had a spacious suite, a refreshing swimming pool, and a food spread that was almost too good to be true—vibrant fresh fruit and vegetables, and the most incredible freshly squeezed watermelon juice every morning included in our hotel stay. James was especially happy to spend time just relaxing in the cool air-conditioned comfort of our room or splashing in the pool, away from the city's sticky heat. He's never been much for hot weather, so we took our time enjoying the hotel's little luxuries. Still, every now and then, curiosity would pull us out for a few adventures beyond the city, eager to explore even more together as a family.

One of the highlights of our trip was revisiting the water puppet show with James, while my sister stayed back at the hotel with the girls. Watching his face light up with delight, just like the first time, made it all worthwhile—though now, nearly six years old, I thought the memories would really stick with him.

One day we set out for the coast to spend some time at the beach. At first glance, the scene was beautiful—bright sun, soft sand, and the endless stretch of blue water calling to us. My sister and I raced to the waves with James, eager to dive in, but our excitement faded quickly. There was so much plastic and debris surfacing in the waves that even our best efforts to clean a bit barely made a difference. It was a shame to find the ocean so polluted in such a stunning place. Instead, we wandered over to watch the men busy at work, sorting, cleaning, and prepping heaps of fresh crabs for market. James was absolutely fascinated by their fast, skillful hands, and their friendly demeanor towards him, turning what could have been a disappointment into one of his favorite memories from the day.

Another adventure took us on an exciting boat ride out to a little island lined with shops and a bustling outdoor restaurant with lively musicians playing traditional Vietnamese music. As soon as we climbed out of the boat, excitement got the better of me—I slipped and took a tumble while holding one of the twins. It was a little embarrassing, but thankfully Eliza was unharmed and only my pride took a hit.

Strolling around the island, we marveled at the enormous jackfruit hanging from the trees—James' eyes were especially large as he gazed at these mammoth fruits. The locals were so friendly and greeted us eagerly, with big smiles and warm curiosity, often stopping to pick up our girls and coo over them. The scene brought back memories of our adoption journey with James, when everyone wanted to hold him as a baby.

I could see the wonder on James' face as he took it all in—the sights, the faces, the feeling of belonging. "Everyone looks so interesting!" he said, his eyes wide with surprise and delight. For the first time, he was surrounded by so many people who looked just like him, and I could tell the experience left a deep impression on his heart.

Another fun outing was our adventure to the Saigon Zoo. It was a bit of a homecoming for James—he'd first visited as a baby and had been smitten with the elephants ever since. This time around, the kids were thrilled from the moment we walked in. Unlike zoos back home, everything felt up close and personal. The animals weren't tucked far away behind fences; instead, they felt almost close enough to reach out and say hello to. The zoo itself had that old fashioned charm, which just added to the fun.

The kids couldn't get enough of watching the animals play and show off their silly antics. They leaned over railings, giggling and pointing at the mischievous monkeys, and stared in awe as the elephants stretched their long trunks over the railing to be fed. Being able to really watch the animals interact made the whole experience that much more magical for them—and for us, too.

Overall, the trip to Vietnam was unforgettable, and we felt genuinely welcomed everywhere we went. Our unique family drew lots of positive attention—from friendly smiles to enthusiastic greetings along the way. James and his bubbly personality instantly connected with so many people; he loved having a vibrant social experience, soaking up every new interaction. The twins were also quite popular. They were a very unique anomaly in Saigon. You don't see a lot of Black people in Vietnam, let alone cute twin baby girls. Everyone who worked at the hotel wanted to hold them and loved snapping photos with the twins. James may have felt a bit jealous, but he certainly received his own share of admiration and affection as well.

On the way back we had a layover in the Seoul airport. It was a lovely place for us to have a layover. Lots of good food and shopping. There was a play area for the kids, free massage chairs, lounge chairs for napping, free showers and toiletries. They even had courtesy buttons to push in the bathroom stalls in case you needed to muffle the sounds made while releasing. Oh, the little touches.

The return flight wore me out. By the time we landed, I had only managed minimal sleep over the past 24 hours and was too exhausted to think straight. As I walked through the airport, it was a challenge for me to form a cohesive sentence when a stranger struck up a conversation with me.

To make matters worse, just as we were leaving the airport after our marathon journey—13 hours on a plane with an 8-hour layover—my sister overheard a group of Black women talking about my daughters. One of them remarked, "If she's going to adopt Black girls, she should at least learn how to do their hair." That comment landed heavy, especially in my completely sleep–deprived state. It echoed in my mind and stung my heart, no matter how hard I tried to shake it off. I know their hair, at just one year old, is still a work in progress—and so am I, learning and doing my best every day. In that moment, all I could think of was how unfair it felt to be judged after such an exhausting journey, and how little people see our lives beyond the surface. But even through the haze, I reminded myself that love, not appearances, is what truly completes a family. Some people will always judge without understanding, but I choose to focus on how far we've come, and how much more we will learn together. This experience has shown me the importance of cultivating a backbone for the many comments that may come our way regarding my girls' hair. It's crucial that I embrace this journey with strength and resilience, and support my daughters with love and understanding as they grow.

Chapter 18

There are two things in life for which we are never fully prepared. Twins.

Have you ever met a twin? Regardless of whether they were identical or fraternal, you can bet that it was a challenge for their parents, especially their mom. I have joined two online groups for twins+. I read about the many stories of these moms, and we can all relate. Sure, there are some pros (they have a playmate, and they are so cute when they are dressed alike), but the cons can be many—and quite frankly, exhausting.

First, there is the shopping. You now must buy two of everything. You can't just buy one toy and expect them to share. Thinking that there is safety in buying two different toys and that they can share is a laughable misstep as well. All toys need to be bought in pairs so as to not disrupt the natural flow of the built-in playmates. The colors can vary according to their likes, but don't create a sibling squabble over sharing the same toy. Keep the peace and heed these words for your own sanity.

Twins can be double the trouble as the saying goes. Luckily, I didn't have the total sleep deprivation that comes from having twins the first eight months of their lives. But it still exists beyond. If one wakes up, you can bet the other will wake, and the playing begins. Getting one back to sleep can be a struggle, but two can be a harrowing battle, especially as they become toddlers. Once they are toddlers, they can climb and move fast. Plus, they feed off each other's energy, which can create some interesting challenges.

Feeding twins can be a challenge for nursing mothers, however, this was not an experience I chose. I could have taken the hormones to produce milk but in vitro supplied me with enough hormones for a lifetime. Feeding them was still a chore, though. As babies, I decided that they could just use the same spoon—they didn't seem to mind. I had to work fast to go back and forth so they wouldn't fuss at me. Once we were home, I fed them one at a time since I only had one high chair. As they became toddlers, I used James' wooden high chair that Papa had bought for us and a light blue booster chair that I had used for James as well. I quickly realized that Zoey would get out of her seat if I put her in the booster. Eliza usually stayed in the booster, so Zoey was the one I strapped into the high chair.

Changing diapers becomes a chore. Many modern moms choose disposable diapers, but this can get expensive when buying for two. I decided to use them only for travel and continued the use of cloth diapers, although I had to buy a lot more to accommodate two babies. Keeping up with cleaning these was a massive job. If it was a poopy diaper, I had to soak the diaper in the toilet, then put on rubber gloves and ring out the diaper—and flush and soak some more. Urine drenched diapers were done similarly, but not quite as messy. Then into the diaper pail until wash time in the washing machine. Then the dryer and folding. Repeat. With twins this is an ongoing chore since there are twice as many.

I developed what is called "mommy thumb," a sharp pain at the base of the thumb that feels inflamed, over the year and a half of doing this process. Between the holding of twins and wringing out diapers, this pain in my thumb remained and still acts up to this day.

Bathing is also an exciting job. Two in the tub can be a fun playtime and double the chance of floating poop. Of course that means take each child out, rinse, hope they don't go again while cleaning the tub, refill, and repeat. I will admit this happened with the other twin on several occasions. It's like monkey see, monkey do. Controlling two kids at the same stage of growth is always a challenge. A sense of humor and a reminder of their blessing in your life are what keep a mama sane.

One of the cutest things that I noticed with the twins was a foreign language that would come out of their mouths that they both used to communicate. This phenomenon is called cryptophasia. Not all twins do this, but about half are said to develop this unique form of communicating during their early years of development. It is quite enduring and hilarious at the same time. I couldn't understand any of it, but they seemed to respond to each other in a knowing way that was so sweet and often entertaining. They still do this at twelve.

Twin Black daughters means double the hair to manage. When I adopted my girls, I knew I would either need to find a hair stylist to do their hair or learn how to do it myself. I was given a referral from a friend of mine at work. This woman invited me over to her home and attempted to teach me how to braid in extensions. It was a completely new experience, but I was game. While she worked on one girl she distracted the other with a video. She had a young daughter herself and that became a distraction for her.

We managed to multitask with keeping our girls entertained and doing hair. She was a sweet and patient young Black woman who normally did adult hair in a salon. This was an angel at work. She was intrigued by our family and the challenge of her task. I had brought the necessary tools to get the job done and was enamored by the technique until we got to the fire portion of the hair. This was a bit scary to me. In order to seal the ends of the extensions she needed to use fire. This was not something I had considered. She insisted that it was safe and the best way to keep the synthetic hair from fraying. I was definitely apprehensive and concerned. But the end result was so beautiful and the girls loved their new hair. This was by far not an easy day, but for the next ten weeks, they had pretty hair and I didn't have to do anything but wash their scalps every few days.

Although the hair was fun and beautiful, I realized I did not have the patience to attempt extensions for my twins on my own. Nor did I have the money to hire someone to do their hair regularly. So, it would be a while before extensions were going to happen again.

Public relations is sometimes an emotional rollercoaster with twins, but even more so with twins that don't look like you. Preparing myself emotionally for the comments and opinions that others may have about my daughters—especially regarding sensitive topics like hair, identity, culture, and yes, racist remarks and acts—is important for both me and my children.

Here are some strategies I chose to use, even for Ethiopian twins:

Educate Yourself

Familiarize yourself with the cultural significance and care associated with different hair types. The more you understand, the better equipped you'll be to navigate conversations and respond to opinions.

Develop a Support Network

Build relationships with other adoptive parents or those from the same cultural background as your kids. They can provide insights, share experiences, and offer emotional support when faced with challenging comments.

Practice Positive Self-Talk

Remind yourself of your worth as a parent and the love and dedication you have for your children. Develop affirmations that celebrate your unique family and your children's beauty.

Role-Play Responses

Anticipate potential comments and practice your responses. This can help you feel more confident when faced with real situations. You can choose to respond with kindness, assertiveness, or even humor, depending on what feels right. When I wanted to be snappy, I went on Facebook and commiserated with the groups for moms of multiples and international adoptive parents.

Set Boundaries

It's okay to establish boundaries regarding comments or opinions that you find disrespectful or inappropriate. Communicate to others that your family is a source of love and respect, and that you expect the same in your interactions.

Focus on Your Kids

Remember that your priority is your children's well-being and happiness. Engage in open conversations with them about identity, hair care, and diversity. Cultivating their self-esteem will help them manage any external opinions.

Stay Calm and Centered

Develop stress-reduction techniques, such as mindfulness, meditation, or deep-breathing exercises. Staying calm during challenging moments can help you respond more thoughtfully. I also try to clear away any bad energy in places we go. Confidence, kindness, and smiles.

Seek Professional Support

If you find yourself struggling to cope with comments or the emotional weight of your experiences, consider seeking support from a therapist or counselor. They can provide tools to help manage your feelings and reactions. Also joining support groups with other international adoption families online or locally can be very helpful. The adoption agency was a good resource for making connections. Even self-help books can come in handy when no one is available.

Celebrate Your Journey

Embrace the beauty of your family and the uniqueness of your children. Celebrate their culture and identity at home, making it a source of pride rather than something to be judged. Learn each other's cultures together. It's an exceptional journey and super interesting and fun for your family.

Model Resilience

Show your kiddos how to handle comments gracefully. By demonstrating resilience and self-acceptance, you can empower them to embrace their identity in a positive light. And if you make a mistake, remember to model love and understanding for yourself.

Ultimately, I needed to remember that you can't control what others say, but you can control how you respond and how you raise your children in a loving and supportive environment.

It is my prayer that people have mercy for mothers of multiples—whether it be offering a helpful hand or a look of acceptance during times of public turmoil. It is my prayer that all judgment of moms, for whatever reason, become understanding and a show of empathy. It is not an easy job. It takes a village, not a villain, to raise tiny humans.

Chapter 19

As I kept juggling the challenge of working outside the home while raising my three young kids, I began to seriously reconsider my options. I had joined a multi-level marketing company and was having some success, but I wanted to take things a step further—maybe even combine it with other areas of health and wellness and become a health and wellness coach. At the same time, what weighed on me most was realizing just how much of myself—and my time—I had poured into educating and caring for other people's children. It really started to hit me that it was finally time to focus on my own kiddos.

The idea of retiring from teaching to become a stay-at-home mom was more than just a passing thought; it was a dream I truly wanted to make happen. Although my husband was not 100%, on board with it, I was convinced that if I took early retirement, we could afford it until I had built my home business. Many coworkers and my dad discouraged this move, but I was determined to be available for my kids whenever they needed me, whether it was for a hug or school activities.

The business I was creating was an integrated approach to health. I had been doing research and went down a rabbit hole and discovered something that struck a nerve. As I had mentioned earlier, my mother had an appendectomy while three months pregnant with me. They had given her a drug that would supposedly ensure that I would survive the surgery. I found a website that described such a drug that was given to women during the 1940s through the early 1970s. Diethylstibestrol (DES) was the drug and had been discontinued when it was linked to cancer and several other problems.

This intrigued me and I began reading more. There were websites about women who had been exposed to this drug in utero. They were called DES daughters. The more I read, the more I saw my life flash before my eyes. These women had a greater risk for infertility. There was a higher risk for ectopic pregnancies and miscarriages.

This was the drug my mom had told me about. This is the drug she had taken when she was pregnant with me. This is the reason I was unable to have a biological child. This! Before I didn't really know why, but this made sense. In that moment, I couldn't shake the feeling that, somehow, all of this was my fault. I was in a dark place, one that I never even considered possible. My mom had told me to stay in good health because of this. Now I felt afraid that I might develop cancer and not be able to take care of my kids. I was in a panic and the anxiety seeped in like never before.

Research into the reproductive health issues associated with DES exposure is extensive for both daughters and sons. For DES daughters there are structural abnormalities. One such anomaly is the prevalence of a T-shaped uterus, which can affect fertility and pregnancy outcomes. Hmmm. I had that. Vaginal and cervical issues also included the presence of conditions such as vaginal adenosis and cervical dysplasia. Yikes!

More research had been done on fertility rates and challenges faced by DES daughters—issues with conception, the use of assisted reproductive technologies, and the increased incidence of ectopic pregnancies and miscarriages. Additional pregnancy-related concerns included increased risk of complications during pregnancy, preterm labor, placental issues, and pregnancy loss. Some of which I had incurred.

Ongoing studies directly link in utero DES exposure to increased risk of clear cell adenocarcinoma of the vagina and cervix, as well as potential links to breast cancer later in life. I had always hated getting breast exams and realized I probably was at risk—and needed to do this more regularly. I would have to tell my doctor to check for these cancers during my yearly exams. My emotional roller coaster would not stop. The rabbit hole had done its damage, and I would be forever scorned. Not knowing for sure if it was me or my husband who had the issue that kept us from being biological parents had helped ease my acceptance, but this opened up a new can of worms. I felt guilt and sadness.

The psychological dimensions were exuding through my being now. I had come to terms with having adopted kids and wouldn't change that for anything. But this knowledge was interference in my head now that was jumping in occasionally and giving me thoughts I did not welcome. I recall instances when seeing blue-eyed, blonde kids with curly hair and wondering—what if? I would shake these thoughts as fast as they came in, but that didn't make them any less real. Guilt percolated through me that I would even have thoughts like this with my amazing kids. The mental anguish of these thoughts surfaced occasionally.

And then something else happened that added to my mental hell.

I was advised that in order to grow my business, I could take out large sums of money from credit cards that had no interest for a year. I had excellent credit, so I was offered a significant amount of money. When asked about my income during the application process, I was told to put down what I was hoping or planning to make, so I estimated $200,000 a year. The advice was then to take out cash from the total credit I was given, so I'd have money on hand both to use and to make the payments back.

But somewhere along the way, I misunderstood the process. I thought I wouldn't have to start paying any of it back until the end of the 12-month period. In reality, I was supposed to be making small payments throughout the year—on ten credit cards. A few months in, I started getting calls from the credit card companies. I felt like an idiot. I had been buying everything I needed for my business, but I hadn't been making those required payments. Suddenly, I was facing serious financial trouble. The mental hell hit me when I was hit with the truth—the managing and understanding of this borrowing went over my head. I realized I had made some mistakes and was in a heap of financial trouble. Something I had never experienced. Instantly, a wave of anxiety flooded over me—my chest tightened, and I felt my breath caught in my throat.

The guilt from the DES, and now financial fall out, weighed heavily on me. I was a wreck. I had three kids, a husband who was navigating a period of personal reflection and life transition, and these anxious thoughts swirling constantly in my mind. I lost "Barbara mode" and anxiety took over my being. I felt the anxiety all the time and was trying to function—and failing. I could barely function and that is when I realized I needed some help. I could not handle this alone. I went through different channels to find this help. I had an energy worker, I meditated, I exercised often, and I started to see signs of a higher power. Some thing was reaching out to me. I could sense it, but I didn't know what it was.

One day I was filled with dread and doubt about where I was going. Suddenly, the unknown became scary, and I felt a tug to go to church. I had grown up in the Methodist church, but being married to an atheist had drawn me away from religion or even the existence of God. Although I had gone on a spiritual journey in my forties, I had not desired returning to Christianity until now. So I went onto the Internet and did some searching. I came across a church in a town nearby, Folsom, CA. There was a video and I clicked on it. The man was the minister of the church and was giving a talk about his marathon run.

This man—thin, not very tall, late forties, Caucasian man—had recently completed the New York marathon and had fundraised over $30,000 for a charity in west Ethiopia. It was near where my girls had been born. It was to be used to build an aqueduct. Currently young girls and women would have to walk several miles to fetch water for their tribe. This journey could be dangerous for several reasons: wild animals, terrain, men who would attack and rape... This story hit me hard. I felt like God was speaking to me and was leading me to this church. I decided to go on the website and found that they had women's Bible study groups during the week. I looked into it and found they also had childcare during the Bible study. And I made it happen.

The group of women seemed nice and I felt some relief while attending the group. I continued to go and decided to check out the church service on Sunday. I enjoyed the music; they had a live band. James enjoyed the Sunday school class. I continued to attend and we became very involved in the church. James even joined the Vacation Bible School that summer. I also went to some marriage seminars and got my husband to attend once. I felt like there was a light and that the unknown was not as scary after all. God was with me, and his Spirit was guiding me out of the darkness I had walked into.

Then something triggered me. I was at a Bible study and the leader of our group brought in literature about various religions. The information described the differences between the sects and even labeled some as cults. Cults have such a negative connotation in our society. The whole conversation did not feel right to me. I was in search of Truth, yet these women were not talking as I expected a Christian should talk. Jesus was an example of how to behave. He was a radical who loved and accepted all. He was not afraid of hanging out with "marginalized" people. He preached love. I was not feeling love at this moment. My uncle had joined the Church of Jesus Christ of Latter-day Saints (LDS) several years before and his wife was a Buddhist. Both of these religions were being called heresy and cults. I knew that was not true. I had studied Buddhism myself and it felt more like a philosophy. The Church of Jesus Christ of Latter-day Saints was never talked about as a cult in my sphere. My mom loved listening to the Mormon Tabernacle Choir. It was my understanding that they were a Christian sect.

I went home and prayed about this and serendipitously, three days later, some missionaries from the LDS church came to my door. My husband called out to me that some young men were at the door and wanted to talk to me about Jesus. He was being facetious. He had been amused with my recent attendance at church and thought it was funny. I, however, welcomed them in and realized this was my chance to learn about the "cult." Was this an answer from God? Had He led them here to answer my questions?

This was the beginning of a journey with the missionaries. What had started out as a learning opportunity turned into some great relationships with people in the church. So now I was attending two different churches. I found the church service in the LDS church to be similar to the Methodist church, more than the other Christian church. It seemed more reverent and less boisterous in their singing and sermons. There was a sense of peace in that.

After about six months of studying with the missionaries—at this point we were studying with sister missionaries—we were again asked if we were ready to be baptized. I had been talking to James about it as we read *The Book of Mormon:*

Another Testament of Jesus Christ. James felt an impression that what we had read was Truth, and I felt strongly about his impressions. He was my "old soul" son, and I respected his beliefs. I had told the missionaries at this moment that we would do it. We were all so happy and pleased.

My husband was not so happy or pleased though. He worried that differences in faith—he is now more of an agnostic—could create tension or distance between us. I already felt like our life was not going as planned and trust in Christ was bringing me out of the dark and into the light. I had finally reached a feeling of release from my anxiety and feeling more joy and happiness in the house. But the happiness was about to be tested by his distrust for "Mormons."

I am grateful to share my journey of faith and the profound reasons behind my decision to join the Church of Jesus Christ of Latter-day Saints. Through my exploration of the church's teachings, I found a strong sense of community, purpose, and a deep connection to Christ's teachings. The emphasis on family, service, and personal growth resonated deeply with my values.

In my experience, the church's message has provided clarity and hope in a sometimes chaotic world. I look forward to continuing my journey of faith and sharing the joy I have found in this remarkable community. I had often had questions about the Bible that didn't seem to match the teachings of the protestant churches. I began to have a sense of coherency with my heart/body and the teachings of The Church of Jesus Christ. The more I learned, the more I felt congruence and comfort in the teachings.

Chapter 20

The new faith I embraced filled our lives with light, healing, and a renewed sense of purpose. Still, our journey continued; practical steps lay ahead. Readoption was going to be necessary for the purpose of changing our kids' names. Readoption is done in front of a U.S. judge after an international adoption has occurred in order to obtain a birth certificate from a state in the U.S.A. We would be receiving California birth certificates for all three of our children. It is also an opportunity to make any name changes legal. They still were legally listed with the names given by their country of origin.

James was already enrolled in school, so it was about time we got it done. Currently their birth certificates, social security, and passports had their birth names. They all knew their original names, but by now, preferred their adoptive names. As to not create confusion in school and medical records, we made the appointment to do this.

It was August of 2015. James was seven and the twins were almost three years old. It was an exciting day to make our family official in all ways. The judge was thrilled to help us out with the process. He loved the richness and complexity of our family structure and reveled in the sweet communication with our kids. Once we received the birth certificates, we could legally change the names on their Social Security cards as well.

With the legal details finally settled and their records in order, we could now focus on James' transition into second grade. I had decided to recommend he be put into a specific Montessori class so he could continue learning through the child-centered, hands-on approach he had thrived in since preschool. Several other moms had done the same and had said the teacher was great. This turned out to be a mistake in many ways. The teacher became pregnant that year. I think this made her a bit more emotional and she was having trouble navigating a challenging child in her class. His name would become a household name and topic as well.

The good thing about the year was that James was referred to speech therapy—not only because English was his second language, but also because he struggled with r's and l's, sounds not found in Vietnamese. The not-so-good-thing was that five students left the class that year due to parents being discontent with the teacher. James did not want to leave though because his best friend was still in the class. He was having a really rough year, and after talking to his teacher with no real improvement, I wrote a letter to the principal. This is the letter I wrote and sent:

> James has had a difficult school year for many reasons. The reasons he has told me throughout the year are as follows.
>
> The teacher yells a lot
>
> Dallas bullies him
>
> The teacher is stressed out
>
> He is not learning anything at school this year because the teacher spends a lot of time getting the class to listen
>
> Doesn't understand why he should go to school, "What's the point of school? I learn more at home."

Dallas did...

The teacher let us out late today because the class wouldn't listen...

We had another substitute teacher today (there were an inordinate amount this year)

Other concerns:

James has had sleep issues: nightmares, waking up at night or early to be with us, not wanting to get out of bed in morning—dreading to go to school.

Experiencing high levels of loss: Deaths of family members and family pets, 5 students pulled from the class to be transferred into other classes, not wanting to move from the class for fear of not being with his friends, 2 friends moved away from Cameron Park, family struggles

Crying and not wanting me to leave the school—wanting me to stay with him in class

Showing little interest in his teacher and his teacher showing little interest in him (He had been very social, loved school, and loved all of his teachers in the past)

He feels left out at school

When I ask, "How was your day?" he generally says "Good," but then when I ask him what was good about it to invite conversation and reflection, he often points out something bad that didn't happen that day rather than good things happening. I find it sad that good means that to a 7-year-old. When I was 7, good was good things happening, not that something bad didn't happen.

At dinner we ask each other what our successes were for the day. Too often James will say something about Dallas. Example: Dallas went home early, Dallas was absent, Dallas didn't sit next to me, Dallas didn't bug me, Dallas didn't bully me... My teacher didn't yell at us today.

He has been very attached to his parents in the past, but the attachment is stronger this year than in the past.

His excitement for school has dwindled—this breaks my heart. I was an elementary school teacher for 20 years and many of my relatives before me worked in various facets of education. Education is important to me, and I hoped to pass this on to my son. I fear he has become disillusioned with school.

What I would like to have the school do to help:

Do not put my son in a class with Dallas ever again.

Get him into a counseling group or one-on-one counseling.

Encourage the love of school.

Put him in a class with a warm teacher who uses positive, strength-based approaches to management; someone who is good with parent communication and makes everyone feel welcome.

The teacher ended up receiving counsel due to several complaints from parents in the first few months. After that, she started displaying student work on the walls and inviting parents to help out in the classroom. While things improved somewhat, I noticed that James' enthusiasm for school had faded. That same year, he worked with the school counselor, who gently encouraged him to find the positives in his school experience. The following year, he was not placed in the same class as Dallas. Although his love of learning remained strong, he gradually lost interest in the institution of public education. Still, what never faded was his affection for the social side of school—his friendships, the laughter, and the sense of belonging he found with his peers continued to light up his days.

Although James lost his zest for school, he kept nurturing friend-ships and developing a sense of teamwork through activities outside the classroom. That summer James joined Little League and enjoyed hanging out with friends. For a seven-year-old, there's nothing quite like the thrill of putting on a matching team uniform, racing out onto the field, tugging on his baseball cap, and pounding on his new leather mitt, ready for action. He seemed to love the playful banter in the dugout, the way kids teased each other and laughed between innings, the high fives after a good play, and a sense of belonging that came from being part of a team. For James it wasn't just about baseball; it was about camaraderie, teamwork, and the happiness of being surrounded by kids who were having fun. And after the challenges of the school year, he felt such relief and freedom to just be himself, away from Dallas, and able to enjoy the simple joys of being a kid.

While James was making memories on the baseball field that summer, life off the field was changing in more subtle ways. My dad started having more medical issues—a reality that while not unexpected at 87, brought new worries and responsibilities. We made several trips to Oregon throughout the summer to check on him and help him out with the house and yard, enjoying the time together while making sure he had the support he needed.

My sister Bonnie joined us for one of the visits. Bonnie worked at Fred Meyer in the Beaverton area, and with a Medford location near my dad's house, we took the opportunity of going shopping with her. We needed to do some back-to-school clothes shopping, and having Bonnie along with us was a real help—thanks to her employee discount at Fred Meyer and the fact that there's no sales tax in Oregon. We were hoping to save quite a bit of money, but unfortunately, our shopping spree was interrupted.

My three kids and I arrived at the store, along with Bonnie and her grandchild Sequoia. I was putting Zoey into a shopping cart when, in a split second, she lost her footing. The next thing I knew, she tumbled out and smacked her head on a metal grate on the floor. The sound of her screams filled the store, cutting right through me. My heart sank and I was instantly flooded with guilt and panic—how could I have let this happen? I scooped her up, barely able to fight back tears of my own, feeling like the world's worst mom for not catching her in time. In that moment, all I could think about was if she would be okay and how helpless I felt watching her in pain.

Here I was in a very White town in Southern Oregon with my toddler crying and screaming in the middle of the store aisle. I was visibly upset, my sister looked stricken, and Zoey was inconsolable. Yet no one stopped to help or see if we were okay. People just walked by—some glancing over, some even looking annoyed or amused. For a moment, I started to wonder if things would have been different if my daughter were White? Would the response have been different? Then my sister quietly voiced what I was too hesitant to say out loud. This was not the first time I had felt this way and deep down, I knew it probably wouldn't be the last. Still standing there, clutching Zoey in my arms, I felt more alone than I expected—or wanted—to feel.

We eventually asked one of the workers to get us some ice, and they brought some over to us. Until we spoke up, they had just stood by, watching hesitantly. Keep in mind, in 2016 only 2.8% of the state's population was Black. Though not all Oregonians were unfavorable towards people of color, there were known white supremist groups in Southern Oregon. Many places in Oregon still had racist names for Chinese, Jewish, Native American, and Black pioneer landmarks. Just a few miles away was Negro Ben Mountain, which was originally called Ni**er Ben Mountain. There were still landmarks and places in Oregon displaying racially insensitive names for Chinese, Jewish, Native American, and Black pioneer landmarks—some even quite offensive. However, people are becoming more aware. Awareness is key to change— and that awareness led to change. An offensive and racially insensitive landmark that existed for years was later renamed to be the Ben Johnson Mountain in 2020, a celebration my girls got to be a part of.

The racial insensitivity from the past became clear again, and I could sense unspoken judgments around us. I did my best to comfort Zoey, and thankfully the ice seemed to soothe her. After a few minutes, her crying subsided, and she nestled into me, still shaken but calmer. Once she seemed okay, we tried to continue our shopping. But out of nowhere, she suddenly threw up—no warning, no complaints. It caught us completely off guard and made me realize how serious her fall might have been. That's when we suspected she might have a concussion. So, we grabbed the kids and headed to the hospital. We got her checked in and set up for an MRI. Sure enough, she was concussed. The doctor assured us she would be okay, explaining that we just needed to keep an eye on her and make sure she didn't overdo it for a while.

Relief washed over us—gratitude rising in the wake of our worry. After what seemed like an eternity of uncertainty, we were able to breathe a little easier. I've always felt that it was my job to shield my children from harm, to somehow protect them from every possible danger. But moments like these remind me that I can't prevent everything—accidents will happen, no matter how closely I watch. What I can do is hold them close, comfort them through the tears and fear, and do my best to see them safely through. With Zoey discharged, we rounded up the kids and left the hospital. Our hearts much lighter, we headed back to the store to finish our shopping, deeply thankful it hadn't been any worse.

After spending some time getting my dad's home and health in order—and ready for school to begin, I felt it was okay to leave. So, we headed back to California in time for James to start third grade. After the previous year I was hoping for a fresh start and a smooth transition with his new teacher, but as we were settling in and James was adjusting to school, I got a call that my father , also named James, ended up in the hospital and we had to head back to Ashland.

We made the long drive back to Oregon as soon as we could. Seeing him so weak, struggling to get his energy back, was hard. He had lost so much weight over the past year and barely touched his food. I tried to get him to eat more, but his appetite was waning. This is often a sign that someone is reaching the end of their life, though I tried not to let myself dwell on that thought. When he was well enough to come back home, there was a flicker of hope he would continue to improve.

Even with that hope, as we packed up our things to return to California, I carried a heaviness in my heart. He'd been through so much lately, and though I tried to reassure myself with his tiny steps forward, worry hung over me—which continued as we drove back home.

School had been in session for two months and James seemed to be doing a little better this year. It was late October when I got another call—my father was back in the hospital. My husband's father had passed away the previous year, and I knew that this might be the last opportunity for my kids to see their only surviving grandfather. Besides, their presence always brightened my daddy's mood. It was important to me to have them come along.

Again, I packed up the kids and took them to Ashland. This time for longer. He wasn't getting any better, and I couldn't bring myself to leave his side. Most days I spent hours by his bedside with the kids in tow, doing my best to balance their needs with my worry for my father. Most of the staff was quite friendly and understanding of my situation; however, there was one nurse who didn't seem too pleased having young children around, and her impatience was wearing on me. Making an already hard situation feel even heavier. He continued to not eat, and his heart was weakening, so, he needed to be moved into the ICU—which made it even more stressful since the children were not allowed to go in. I told my sister I felt that his condition was worsening and that it could be close to the end of his journey here on Earth.

Luckily, my sister was able to get time off from work and she drove down from Portland, which helped me with the kids. My dad had been diagnosed with congestive heart failure. He had not been eating very much and had lost a lot of weight. He was down to about 120 lbs. and was too weak for surgery. We kept trying to get him to eat to build up his strength, but when people are ready to die, their appetite fades and they refuse food; without nourishment, the body starts to feed off its organs.

He was moved out of ICU once his vitals were stable. The doctor prescribed morphine regularly, so my father was not very coherent. It was evident he was not going to get better, so we started to plan for hospice. He wanted to be in his own home, so we ordered a hospital bed. After it was delivered, the ambulance took my father home and helped carry him upstairs to his room.

Once we were settled in at home, it was clear my father didn't have much time left. Despite everything, he told me he wanted to have a going away party, a last gathering to say goodbye. Sad, but sweet. We invited all of his friends to come visit one last time. We made Bloody Marys, his favorite drink. He had a hard time drinking it, but with help, he was able to get some of it down through a straw. He was not always lucid, drifting in and out of the conversation, but his friends' faces would brighten when they saw him, and each shared a favorite story. The love in the room was over-whelming, and while there was laughter, there was a heavi-ness too—a sense of letting go. It was a bittersweet day, filled with memories, tears, and the kind of connection that only comes when you know time is short. I'll never forget the way everyone came together for him, making his end days full of comfort and warmth.

The next day he was mostly unconscious with occasional lucidness. James had been out of school for a week, and I was hoping to get home for Halloween. Bonnie wanted me to stay, so I decided family was more important than school. We decided to stay. At one point my father awoke to say he loved me and was quickly out again.

It was October 30th and tomorrow would be Halloween. We went to Goodwill to find costumes for the kids. James fashioned a pirate, Zoey created a cat costume, and Eliza found a princess dress. The kids would participate in their first Ashland Halloween parade the next day.

That night the two of us took turns waking up to check on Dad so we could give him morphine. It was about 4 a.m. when Bonnie tapped me on the shoulder to wake me up and tell me that she thought Dad had passed. I awakened immediately and went upstairs to check on him. He was not breathing. I grabbed his hand to check his pulse; Bonnie held his other hand. The hand I was holding was still warm and I felt a slight squeeze. Bonnie said his other hand was cold. I could not find a pulse and realized he was gone. I felt as though he waited for me to come to him before he let go completely. It was a tender mercy to sense this and a great comfort at a time of great loss.

My sister and I were now orphans. My father had died on Halloween. This was the second parent we had both watched die. I couldn't help but notice the weird coincidences. Mom had died Friday, October 13, same as her dad, and now My dad had died on the reverse of 13, October 31—Halloween. This was so creepy. Here I was on Halloween, with my dead father and three kids who were still expecting to go to the Halloween parade and trick or treating. I couldn't shake the strangeness of the haunting mirrored dates. This was also the date of one of my miscarried twins. Was there some meaning to this or does God just has a weird sense of humor?

We woke up the kids so they could say goodbye to their Papa. We then called hospice to have his body removed. It was all so emotional as they carried his body out and dismantled the hospital bed. I could still feel his presence even after his body was gone.

That afternoon, Ashland was having its yearly Halloween parade. With a sick feeling in my stomach and a determination to give my kids a fun Halloween, we got everyone in their costumes and walked downtown. It was cold enough to be coat weather, yet the sun was shining. The streets were crowded with kids and adults in loads of creative and ominous costumes. It was such a surreal feeling as though I was tripping on drugs or in a misty dream. The feeling of losing your dad and all these terrifying costumed people walking around in creepy character was sinister. I was in a veritable quandary. I continued to guide my kids in this unreal trance.

I felt uneasy about keeping James out of school for another week, but sometimes life takes you places you are not planning. We needed to start sorting through my dad's belongings, prepare his obituary, close out his accounts, and plan for his memorial. My sister Becky was in China during the last week and we had to contact her to let her know Dad had died. She flew to Seattle a few days later and drove down with her daughter and her family. The family was all in Ashland and we were to have the service on November 6.

Planning my dad's memorial service was heavier than I could have imagined, though God was with me—that helped me more than anything. I didn't have the luxury of spiritual guidance with my mom's passing. I wrote his obituary and sent out the announcement, choosing the conference room at the Southern Oregon University library where my dad had been a psychology professor for about 30 years.

I knew I needed to put together a slideshow presentation for the memorial, so I retreated into his bedroom where it was quiet. Being in his room, surrounded by his familiar things, the weight of his loss heavy in the air—I could feel his presence. I felt a quiet calm as I sifted through old family photos, choosing and arranging each one, letting the memories wash over me. I picked out music to accompany the slideshow—songs that reminded me of him, melodies filled with feeling and love. It was both comforting and heart-wrenching; every picture and song brought me closer to him, even as I faced the reality of his absence.

The next day, at the SOU library where we held the memorial service, I felt a deep swell of emotion watching friends, family, and former colleagues gather to honor his life. As the slideshow played, I saw people smile, laugh, and even shed a tear or two—each image and tune stirring memories and emotions throughout the room. It was comforting to see the love he had spread throughout his life, reflected in the faces of everyone gathered.

With the memorial service now behind us, we returned home, carrying both the sadness of loss and the warmth of his memory. James needed to return to school, and Michael to work.

For the next month, Bonnie and I went back and forth to help sort while Becky stayed in Ashland. There were 87 years' worth of belongings to go through, and though it was a big task, it was surprisingly cathartic. We found ourselves laughing at some of the quirky things Dad had held onto—he never liked to let go of anything, just in case he might need it someday. Each discovery, whether it was a funny memento or a long-hidden secret, brought new stories and sometimes even a few surprises. As we reminisced about the good old days, we found comfort in the shared laughter, the occasional tears, and the unexpected pieces of his life we uncovered along the way.

As the weeks went on, Bonnie made a suggestion that caught me by surprise: she suggested that my family move into Dad's house and live there free until we got back on our feet. At the time I had accumulated quite a bit of debt, and my business simply wasn't as successful as I'd hoped—it felt like I was on the verge of giving up. Bonnie's idea seemed like just the opportunity we needed to get a fresh start. By selling our house in Cameron Park, I could pay off my debts. We had often talked about moving back to Ashland but could not afford the real estate—now it could become a reality. Most of our family was in Oregon and Bonnie had been hinting for some time that we should move back. We had also discussed moving away from California due to a law that passed making vaccines mandatory. I refused to let James get anymore vaccines after his bad reaction from his previous vaccines.

After consideration, we decided to do it. I asked James where he wanted to have Christmas, and he wanted to be at his Papa's. That was it, we would move to Ashland for Christmas and start school after winter break. It seemed like a logical transition time into his new school.

Over the next month it was a scramble to pack up our lives and prepare for the move to Ashland. Many church members, along with several other friends, were incredibly helpful—assisting with packing, cleaning, and loading the U-Haul, and offering much needed support. Thanks to their generosity and hard work, we managed to complete everything within a week and were soon on our way to Ashland.

When we first arrived in town, we were immediately welcomed by neighbors, and, to our delight, several church members even showed up to help us unload the U-Haul truck—on Christmas Eve no less. We had our Christmas in Ashland.

My husband would return to California and prepare the house for sale and continue to work at his job. He would come up to see us every two weeks until the house was sold and closed.

James did not get to start school after break because there was a snowstorm, but we sure had fun building snowmen and having snowball fights. Once school started, he was thrilled with his new teacher and made friends fast. It felt like everything was falling into place. In May, the house sold, and my husband was in Ashland to stay. On to new adventures. The scariest part was knowing that I had just moved my family to a town that was still very White, even though it was considered progressive. That made me worry about how my kids would feel and if they would have a sense of belonging growing up in Ashland. Thankfully, the university and Shakesperean Festival brought in people from all over, adding some much-needed diversity to the community. It was reassuring to know that my kids wouldn't be the only people of color in town.

Chapter 21

Building a new life in Ashland was both scary and exciting. I wished I had grown up in Ashland, but since my parents divorced when I was a toddler, my mom wanted to go back to Portland. So now I had an opportunity to bring up my babies in this beautiful valley, nestled between the Cascades and Siskiyou mountains ranges.

Home of the Oregon Shakespeare Festival and Southern Oregon University, Ashland had some culture and diversity. Ashland would provide a close-knit community, family-oriented activities, and exposure to arts and nature. The school district was in the top five in Oregon and fostered creativity with a balance of strong academics. Crime was low and people were friendly... At least that had been my experience.

Mt. Ashland was a thirty-minute drive from Ashland, which was great since James and I were avid skiers. I would teach my girls on the same mountain on which I learned as a kid. The saying goes, "If you can ski Mt. Ashland, you can ski anywhere." Mt. Ashland has several intermediate runs and many advanced black diamond runs—but only one easy run. On a clear day, you can see Mt. McLoughlin and Mt. Shasta, with endless miles stretching through the Cascades and Siskiyou mountains. The most breathtaking view, an absolutely glorious site.

I loved coming here during the holidays from school to visit my father. I loved it so much I had moved here to attend college and graduate school. Now we were back, and I loved it even more. I had experienced enough city life and a small arts-driven town with natural beauty was a bit of solace in a time when I felt pulled between making money and being a totally present mom. Living in my dad's house was familiar, but not easy. We went from 3,300 square feet with a two-car garage and a large backyard to 1600 square feet, no garage, and a tiny backyard. Our plan was to enlarge and remodel the kitchen and add an extra bedroom and dining room. But for now, it was necessary to have a storage unit. Our things could not fit in the house considering I was still going through my dad's 87 years of memorabilia and files. Over the years I helped him organize and purge, but there was still so much to sort through.

I could still feel his presence now and again while in his old bedroom. It was oddly comforting, especially since my husband was still in California. Sometimes the lights would start flickering or my computer would randomly play a song from his memorial slide show. I was consoled by these things, knowing that he was looking out for us from the other side of the veil. I felt that same pleasantness when my mother had died. Weird electronic anomalies and songs from her service playing out in public or on the radio when I needed consoling. James would tell me things when he was a toddler about my mom that he would not have known. I was so enamored that my mom was communicating with her grandson after all. It brought me joy that she knew I had succeeded in creating a family.

As we started settling into our new home in Ashland, we quickly realized that there was more going on beyond its picturesque small town charm. Even though crime was still much lower than in bigger cities, it wasn't completely absent, and issues like racism, prejudice, and judgment sometimes revealed themselves. Ashland was still working on bringing equity, diversity, and inclusion (EDI) into its professional circles, through training and awareness. That was something we'd already grown used to back in Sacramento, so it stood out to us right away.

James had experienced some microaggressions and racism in school from both staff and students. A student said he should be using chopsticks while he was eating rice at lunch. Students often asked him if he was Chinese. The staff assumed he was good at math. I was aware that Asians were considered the "model minority" by many Whites and were expected to act as such. When James was not acting accordingly, it was an issue that seemed bigger than it really was. He was a boy trying to be a kid in a White world. What I didn't realize was that he had a neurodiverse brain and thus his actions were normal for him. I think it was never thought of by his educators due to the unconscious thinking that he couldn't have ADHD because he was the "model minority." It wasn't until high school that it finally came up.

The following school year EDI was beginning to emerge in the Ashland schools. A timely need, especially for my girls, since they would be entering school soon. Black children often face inequities in schools, and I was determined to advocate for my children so they would feel supported and valued. Oregon Department of Education had issued grants for Black students, and Southern Oregon had a large enough population of Black students in their schools to qualify. The grant enabled a team called SOBAASS, Southern Oregon Black and African American Student Success. Together with other parents of Black/African American students, we would gather monthly to discuss target goals, issues, and racism in the schools that needed to be addressed.

This group led to some much needed change in awareness and curriculum implementation of BIPOC (Black, Indigenous, People of Color) culture and history. The big goal was to address the elephant in the room—systemic racism. It was also to ensure a place of dignity and belonging for all, including marginalized populations. I was thrilled to be a part of this for my children and all kids in Southern Oregon. It was also a great way to become connected with the community.

In the beginning stages of SOBAASS, the team spent time deliberating on what changes needed to be made in our schools. A group and website became the next goal for the community. Several hours were spent developing goals for a website. We played around with different ideas for the name and content. One of the parents was a web developer. As a team, we helped to design the site, and he did all the development using our collective ideas. An organization was formed from these meetings in 2018—BSOA, Black Southern Oregon Alliance. This group had a vision to help the BIPOC community become more independent and have a real stake in the overall community, both socially and economically.

Two opportunities have spawned from BSOA partnering with Southern Oregon University, SOU. The first being Black Youth Leadership Summit, which has continued for seven years. This is one day of classes and activities for 3rd-12th grade Black students to attend. At the beginning, only a few dozen students attended; now in 2025, 350 students attended. My daughters have benefited from this day for several years now. It has been a great way for them to connect with the Black community.

The other opportunity is the Black Youth Summer Institute at SOU. This is a week-long camp for students who have completed 7th-12th grade. The summit offers classes, lectures, cultural experiences, and recreational activities. Students get to engage with Black and African American leaders to explore topics of culture and heritage. Next summer Eliza and Zoey will get to attend. They are very excited to spend a week engaged in learning with other Black/African American students from around Oregon.

Another organization that grew over the years and is led by Black parents who we met from SOBAASS is called BASE, Black Alliance & Social Empowerment. The catalyst for this group was propelled by the George Floyd killing in Minnesota during the pandemic. It is so wonderful to have a community for my daughters to be a part of in this White region. There are no Black neighborhoods, but there are a few thousand Blacks scattered throughout the valley that can now come together to be a strong community and be great role models for my daughters and each other.

BASE has received grants and has started several youth activities that have benefited my daughters. It started as an online AfroScoutz community and morphed into BASE youth, BASE girlz, and BASE boyz. They have several activities such as dance, drumming, martial arts, art, coding, field trips, events and mentorship. Each year there is a Juneteenth celebration in which my girls perform a dance routine at Pear Blossom Park in Medford. They hold a yearly Kwanzaa Celebration at the Ashland Armory and an MLK Jr. commemoration in Ashland where they also have the opportunity to perform their dance routines and speak.

Many of the Black youth in Southern Oregon are adopted by White families or of mixed race and feel a place of belonging and dignity thanks to all the people who help make BASE successful in welcoming Blacks and creating community. The organization has made great strides in connecting to the police force and the historical society to create aware-ness into the inequalities and racism that African Americans endure in this State. With allies in Southern Oregon, they are creating a safe space.

The Oregon Shakespearean Festival, OSF, has in recent years embraced IDEA, Inclusion, Diversity, Equity, and Access/Accessibility. This has translated into more People of Color involved in the productions. It has been great to take my son to a play with a mostly Asian American cast, and my daugh-ters to see the leading role of several plays be an African

American woman. This also brings more diversity and awareness to Ashland.

Being a university town also brings diversity to our town. The athletic department has partnered with the elementary school to create mentorship programs. The athletes come from various cultural backgrounds. One of the events held at SOU each year is the Black Youth Leadership Summit. This is a full day of activities for Black students in the Southern Oregon community. There is also a yearly Asian Student Union dinner during Lunar New Year.

I was so skeptical about moving here, but it has truly been a blessing to have these things happening during my children's childhood here in Ashland, Oregon. I am so grateful to all of those who have love in their hearts to make it all happen. God is good.

Another wonderful outcome of Ashland's focus on equity and inclusion is that it created space for affinity groups in the schools; in fact, when my daughters started elementary school, the Black Student Union was formed. It's been nice that they have access to a group they can develop unity with. It has helped them feel empowered to express concerns and problems faced in school and become leaders for change in their school. This has also brought Black History and history of other marginalized groups to become part of the school's curriculum and culture. It is great to see more allies joining in their fight. Martin Luther King Jr.'s dream of little Black children and little White children holding hands as sisters and brothers is becoming a reality here. One step at a time, little by little, progress is being made.

There have been times we experienced various levels of racism in Ashland. The most in our face, though, was when we were renting a movie. We were standing outside the 7-Eleven looking at the Redbox rental kiosk. It was just me and the twins when they were five years old. We were looking at the family movie options when a short, thin, white man with grey hair and piercing blue eyes spit at my foot. I would say he was probably in his late 50s or early 60s. I looked up and he was staring at us with severe intensity. I realized that this was no accident. This was by far the most blatant act of racism we had encountered. The man turned and walked into the store.

I would say I was shocked, but I had been expecting a day like this would eventually occur. Both my daughters looked at me and asked why that man had just spit at us. I looked down at their sweet young faces and began with asking them if they remembered our talks about racism and they shook their heads. I then explained, "This man is not well and had been taught to hate."

We continued to gaze at the movie options and made our choice. The man then exited the 7-Eleven with a Big Gulp and proceeded to take off the lid. He then held on to the cup and threw the soda as it went streaming through the air towards us. It splashed on the ground and up onto us. He then grinned and walked back into the store.

Zoey asked why he did that and I explained to my girls that he was a sick man who needed our prayers. As he walked back out of 7-Eleven with a refill, Eliza approached him with a picture of Jesus and handed it to the racist man. She proceeded to let him know that we would pray for him. He smiled and took the picture, said thank you, and that he loved Jesus. We then got into our car to leave.

This racist, hateful man was not finished though. He came over to my car and went on a rant, telling me how I was going to hell for mixing races. He continued by quoting things that were not actually in the Bible. I respectfully told him I did not agree and that we would pray for him. I then reached down to press the button to roll up my window and drove away.

We knew that following Jesus meant praying for our enemies and loving our neighbors, but in moments like this, it was incredibly hard—especially when I saw someone treating my daughters with such blatant racism. Honestly, part of me just wanted to lash out in anger. I was dumbfounded but did not want to perpetuate hate in front of my sweet girls.

This happened the day before a white supremacist march was scheduled up in Portland, Oregon, which may have given the man the audacity to behave as he had. We then drove to the police station. Why I didn't just call 911 while it was happening is beyond my understanding, but here I was at the station. It was after 5:00 p.m. on a Friday so the station was closed until Monday morning. We would have to wait. So we went home and prayed for our enemy and discussed his sickness. To this day, we all remember it clearly.

Monday morning, I went to the police station to file a police report about the incident and was told I could have called 911 at the time of the occurrence. Live and learn. I was glad to hear that the Ashland police would have our backs if this ever happened again. They told me they would check the surveillance camera at the store to find the man we described. We never heard back. Not surprised.

James did not have an Asian Student Union to help empower him, but he did want to be an ally to his sisters and good friend, Jackson. He went to the BSU meeting and was told he had to leave because he wasn't Black. He had to sit in the hallway and wait for the meeting to end. The irony was the two women who were running the BSU that year were White. One of the other parents heard this confrontation and was furious. When I went to pick up my kids she told me what had happened. I could not believe this could happen, but it did. These women for whatever reason felt empowered to lead the BSU as Whites and to exclude a young Asian ally, brother, and friend. I felt so forlorn along with him.

I decided it would be good to start an Asian Student Union. The support from the school was low, as was the Asian population. It wasn't until James moved to his middle school in sixth grade that we made this a reality. I was White, but I became the ASU leader, along with my son. We had the support of the school and a larger Asian American population. We expanded to include Pacific Islanders and all students of Asian descent and ancestry. We even included student allies to join in the meetings.

It was a very exciting and bonding experience for us, and then the world closed down. The global illness had become a growing concern, and by March of 2020, the pandemic was declared. The schools were closed and the rest is history.

Chapter 22

As a parent in this century, I thought the biggest hurdle was smart devices. But then came the pandemic, for which this generation would forever be changed. In the beginning, the pandemic closures seemed like an extra vacation, but the media frenzy that ensued was creating a panic throughout the world—and a divisiveness that would last for years.

My daughters seemed to meld into this online schooling with much less issue than my son. James was able to engage in the online video game frenzy with his friends, but he slowly slipped out of engagement of his academics online. This was partly due to his need to be social but also his neurodiverse brain being understimulated by online school.

Fall of 2020, James' seventh grade year had started. Online distance learning was still in force, and I had been called to teach. There had been a grass fire that started on September 8th, 2020. The Alameda fire swept through parts of Ashland, and the neighboring towns of Talent, Phoenix, and parts of South Medford. About 2,800 structures, including 600 homes, were destroyed in the fire. Most of the homes were in Talent and Phoenix, Oregon. This added salt to the wound of the pandemic for the community. Phoenix/Talent School District had been given permission to have in person learning due to the destitution caused by the fires and the massive loss of homes for the community. It was a way to bring some normalcy back into the lives of the children.

I had been praying for the families impacted by the fire and how I could be of assistance. I had a prompting to check the substitute listing that I had abandoned after the pandemic started and my kids were left at home and needed my supervision. When I looked at the job listings, there was one for a full-time, in-house substitute teacher. I called and was hired.

This created an issue though. What would happen to my kids and their schooling if I was not there? Since James was old enough to be at home with his sisters, I entrusted him to keep them on task for school as well as himself. Their dad had a job that allowed him to work remotely part of the day and the flexibility to come home if needed. I would be home by 3:30 p.m. to take over.

This seemed to be working out until I realized that James had just about abandoned school. I couldn't blame him. Distance learning was far from ideal, and incredibly frustrating between the technical challenges and the lack of student engagement. He had figured out how to make it appear as though he was attending class while simultaneously playing video games. He was learning skills, just not the distance learning skills intended by the school. I realize remote learning was put into place because of all the rules during the pandemic, and maybe for some it was helpful. But honestly, it just wasn't the best fit for many children, including ours. So much for seventh grade.

My work at the elementary school was not always plentiful. There were days when I was quite frankly bored and searching for work. But when someone got sick or needed to take time off, I was there and ready to take over. These were the days I enjoyed the most. There were two months when I got to teach a second-grade class, and I felt like I was a real teacher again. The downside was that wearing a mask while teaching makes it difficult to convey emotion and to always be clearly understood. I was also going through menopause, and the mask made my periodic hot flashes worse. So I carried a fan that worked by plugging it into my phone. The students thought that was cool.

During the pandemic, our marriage went through a rough patch. There were a lot of broken promises and lingering doubts, and with all the added stress, it became harder and harder to move forward together. The distance between us only seemed to grow as the pandemic wore on. Over time, we grew apart, and I had realized things were not going to get better. I began planning for a separation and asked the school administrators and colleagues to write me recommendation letters. I also talked to a legal team and became educated on next steps, if necessary.

The more we argued, the more I could see it affecting our children in negative ways. I had been married for almost 30 years and was not seeing a path that I would want to continue for the next 30 years. I was exhausted and couldn't do it anymore unless a miracle occurred and change happened. Life doesn't always play fair, but somehow, we seem to always get to where we need to be.

On November 23, 2020, a tragedy occurred at the Stratford Inn Hotel. One of the structures that burnt down during the Almeda fire was the local Burger King. A young man who worked there was now unemployed and homeless. He was a 19-year-old Black youth who had attended Ashland High School and currently staying at the inn. Another man had been displaced after the fire and was living at the Stratford Inn as well. He was in the parking lot playing music in the early hours of the morning when a 47-year-old White male came outside to complain about the music. There was an argument that ensued.

The White man pulled out a gun and shot and killed the young Black man.

This was a tragic moment that had been exemplified by the murder of a Minnesota Black man, George Floyd, who had been killed by police officers earlier that year in May. The killing outraged citizens and gave rise to national protests. Portland, Oregon, had been a leader in the protests against racism and police brutality. These protests went on for several months in Portland, which gained national attention from May to October. The world was getting even crazier.

Community leaders organized a candlelight vigil at the courthouse in Medford. This was a wake-up call for Whites living in "progressive" Ashland. Racism and hate crimes are real. The high school art students created a memorial mural painting of the young man that was killed that stated, "Rest in Power." A "Say Their Names" memorial was also erected at Railroad Park where over 100 T-shirts with names of people killed by racists and police were hung along the fence line.

This memorial was repeatedly vandalized and eventually completely restored in 2024. Our family and friends got together to create eight of the shirts. Then on June 22, 2025, a new monument was unveiled as a permanent Black Lives Matter commemoration.

Something else that came out of all this was a small group who came together to start a community where citizens could meet to discuss racism and how to end its presence here. The group is called Ashland Together. They organize meetings, workshops, and educational talks to educate and bring together community members for change in creating racial and social equity. It's another great way to get my family involved in building a better future, and we try to attend events when possible.

A few months later, I was called for two interviews at Medford schools. One was as a math teacher at a middle school, and the other was at an elementary school teaching a 4/5th grade split. The elementary school Zoom interview was scheduled first, and I was offered the job, so I canceled the other interview. I was so excited because I needed to be employed; by now I had filed for divorce, and was needing permanent employment.

The school was very nice and the staff seemed welcoming. The school year had already started when they realized they needed to make the fourth and fifth grade classes smaller. I was to start out the school year two weeks in. The four classroom teachers would move 6 of their students into my class. The students were already settled into their new school year and were going to be moved into a new class again, but this time with kids from another grade level. This was a difficult job to walk into on many levels.

The global pandemic, mandatory masks, a reorganization of kids into an arrangement they did not ask for—new teacher, new classroom, new peers, and fourth graders who were afraid to be with older fifth graders, and fifth graders who looked at the fourth graders as little kids. Plus, I had a number of "difficult" kids in the mix. I was determined to make it work though.

It was about two weeks in when I got a phone call from my uncle in California. Uncle Bill had made me his executor since he had no kids and his wife was dead. He told me he was in the hospital again and needed me to come down to help. I had just started this challenging teaching position and now I was having to take time off already. I booked a flight for Thursday night and planned to miss just one day, Friday. I would fly back Sunday night. I called my sister and asked if she could meet me. I was afraid this time was serious. She agreed, so I made arrangements and hopped on my flight.

What started out as a weekend changed in the early hours of September 19. My uncle had been moved from the hospital into hospice at his home. He had been dealing with both pulmonary fibrosis and prostate cancer for a few years and recently gotten a coronavirus booster shot. I feel as though he was too weak to handle the vaccine, and it just pushed his health further over the edge. We set up a hospital bed in his living room and called the bishop to give him a priesthood blessing.

We had been given morphine to administer if needed. I asked him if he wanted to take the morphine to ease his discomfort. He said yes and it helped him to sleep. He was out cold and making wheezing noises that kept me from dozing off completely. I had been monitoring him while half sleeping on his pull-out futon couch next to his hospital bed and realized he had stopped making the wheezing noises. I checked for his breath and then his pulse. There was none. I woke up my sister and we determined he had passed on. We called hospice and they came to get his body about an hour later. It was Sunday morning, and I realized I had a lot of work to do. We would have to take the following week off to close out his life and prepare his obituary and funeral services. Once again, my sister and I were together during the death of a loved one.

I felt bad for my class, but life, or death, happens. We can't control our world, just surrender, and move forward. I got busy and ordered the cremation, sent out his obituary, contacted friends and family, set up the funeral, and chose a tombstone. Since Uncle Bill was a member of the Church of Jesus Christ of Latter-day Saints, we were allowed to use the church building for his memorial service and several members helped to organize food, speakers, flowers, and music. The funeral was held at the cemetery on Friday with a flag ceremony since he had been in the Navy as a young man. His brother and family flew in Friday night and we held the memorial on Saturday afternoon. It turned out to be a lovely service. My husband had driven the kids down to attend. The girls even sang a sweet primary song, "I Am a Child of God" at the service.

Over the next few months, life was very complicated. I had to continue to work on closing out my uncle's estate, deal with the pandemic issues, and begin the divorce proceedings. But our church provided much needed comfort and support.

Being part of our church filled our lives with fun, purpose, and so much togetherness. This was a great comfort and help over the following difficult months in our lives. So many great activities kept my kids busy—everything from singing and games to dances, camps, service projects, and youth conferences. My kids have made close friends and learned leadership by collaborating, helping others, and just having a blast together.

Working side by side on service projects—like caring for the church pear farm and picking pears for those in need of food—has helped my kids see how good it feels to make a difference. During the wildfires in Ashland and other surrounding areas, there was so much devastation. Our church joined forces with other community organizations to offer help and support during this difficult time. The church helps anyone who's struggling, which taught our family the real meaning of charity and compassion.

We've also grown together in practical ways—with classes on parenting, money skills, emotional resilience, and more. There's support for whatever life brings, and my kids see adults and teens looking out for each other.

It has been several years since we have been involved with the church, and it has given my children a great foundation for strong moral striving and the ability to forgive and accept others. I've loved seeing my kids inspired to be kind, positive, and open-minded. And as a mom, I've found encouragement and support in the church's Relief Society, which builds up women as leaders, learners, and friends—something I used to think wasn't possible in organized religion. Here, husbands and wives are seen as equals who share the load of raising a family and supporting each other.

From the silly moments at church socials to the deeper feeling of belonging and purpose, this church has brought laughter, comfort, and hope. My kids are growing up surrounded by wholesome goodness, friendship, and inspiration. For our family, church isn't just a place to go on Sundays—it's where we find joy, support, and a sense of being part of something bigger.

Section 7

Forging a New Path

There's something both terrifying and freeing about starting over. After years of feeling stuck, I found myself at the edge of a brand-new road—one I hadn't expected, and definitely hadn't planned for, but one I knew I needed to take. With every step, I was learning how to trust myself again, how to dream, and how to shape a life that felt honest and lighter. This new journey wasn't easy, and there were plenty of doubts, but for the first time in a long time I started to believe there really could be something better waiting down the road.

Chapter 23

Being back in the classroom after years away had not been an easy transition with all that was going on in the world, but nothing compared to the emotional weight I carried outside of work. As November approached, I found myself juggling lesson plans by day and the logistics of divorce by night. When my lawyer sent a process server to deliver the divorce papers to Michael, it became painfully real—there was no turning back. This wasn't just a difficult chapter for me, or even for Michael, but for our children too. The sense of upheaval touched every part of our lives, each of us searching for an anchor in this time of uncertainty.

By Thanksgiving week, I had come down with symptoms of the virus and was relegated to my bedroom for the next ten days. My school expected me to do Zoom conferences, but I was too sick to be presentable. Life was full of bad timing lately.

I went back to my uncle's house during Christmas break with the kids. I had so much work to do to get his house ready to sell. He was a man who didn't get rid of things. Some people would say he was a hoarder of sorts, so there was plenty to sort through and get rid of. I would have to come back a couple more times to get rid of everything—several dump trucks full of garbage and recyclables that he had collected over the years. Once all of that was done, I hired people to come in and paint, repair, and clean up the place. It was like a second full time job.

A few months later, the virus got my son, and I caught it a second time. He was pretty sick, but I mostly just had a cough. I felt as though I was looking like a failure in my job by now. I had missed a lot of work, and it was my first year in the district. I was hopeful I would keep my job but a bit worried. Most everything had been out of my control though.

By May I received word that I would need to transfer to a different school because enrollment was down and I was the last one hired. I had to choose a position at one of five schools that had an opening. The caveat was I had to decide that day. During lunch, I interviewed several teachers about the various schools. I chose a third-grade position at a school that would add an additional 10-15 minutes onto my commute. Sad to be leaving my awesome classroom with a great view of the mountains, but thankful I would still have a job. The school year was coming to a close, and I needed to start packing for the move to a new school.

The divorce was now finalized and I would have custody of the kids. We were still living in my father's home; however, by now Michael and I had bought it out from my sisters. I had six months to either buy it out from him or we would have to sell it.

When I had started teaching, I had to move into a new class-room at the first school. After that I had to move everything out of my uncle's house. And now that I had to change schools, I moved everything into a new classroom at the new school. Moving into my new classroom was the third move in the past year. The new classroom didn't have a great view; however, it did have a small, adjoining room that I turned into a library niche with lots of pillows I kept from my uncle's house. I decorated the class in a jungle theme with monkeys (my favorite animal) and named us Robertson's monkeys. The kids loved it.

Meanwhile, my kids were also starting school. The girls were now in fourth grade and in the same class together for the first time officially (if we don't count sitting next to each other at home during Zoom class). James was starting high school. He finally seemed truly excited again about school. James is such a social kid and he was looking forward to hanging out with all his friends and making new friends. He is that kid who seems to know everyone in town because he is so friendly and remembers everyone's name.

The excitement soon ended about three weeks in when a high school student died by suicide. This was a kid that James knew and who was very close friends with several of James' good friends. James has a lot of empathy and wanted to be a support for all his friends. The school did not handle the incident with best practices in mind. There was no plan intact beforehand. The school seemed to scramble to figure out how to handle the issue as a school, and thus he and other students were extremely affected by this tragedy. They found comfort in each other. Nonetheless, this tragic event had soured the vibe of the school.

As the school year continued, other issues began to arise. James found himself under scrutiny when he and a Jewish friend were jokingly making racist jokes about each other. Although James saw this as a way to make light of stereo-types—something he often saw comedians doing on social media—others were bothered by their remarks. For James, joking about his own identity served as a defense mecha-nism; as a minority in a predominately White population, it was his way of taking control of the narrative and preventing stereotypes from bothering him. However, those around him didn't always understand his intentions. Instead of seeing it as self-deprecating humor, some students perceived it as offensive or inappropriate, bringing up concerns about their impact on students who had different views.

Later that year he had been called into the office because someone told a staff member that James had a pocketknife. In his mind, a pocketknife was a tool. Though he would never threaten anyone with it, he did admit he carried it, saying he might use it for self-defense if he truly needed to. Given the heightened concerns around school safety these days, the administrator took the situation seriously. As a result, James received a two-day in-school suspension.

James couldn't help but feel singled out by the situation, especially since he knew another student who had also been found with a pocketknife—but only received lunch deten-tion. That same teen had been suspended twice before for drug use at school. To James, the consequences didn't seem equitable. He didn't understand the reasoning behind the different responses and wondered if being one of the few non-white students at school might have been a factor.

The irony is that the night before I saw his pocketknife in his belt and asked if he had taken it to school. He told me yes, and that he was cutting an apple with it in front of the prin-cipal who said nothing. I scoffed and said that I doubted the principal saw it and said nothing. I then warned him not to have a pocketknife at school. He claimed I jinxed him by saying that. I said he should have listened to me.

At this point, I'm thinking that raising a teenage boy is not going to be easy. I wished that a hug would make it all better, but he wasn't six anymore. In fact, hugs were a thing of the past. He had decided when he got into middle school that hugging his mom was no longer acceptable. So here we are, a year after the pandemic and divorce—with a rocky start to high school. Pull up your bootstraps mom, it's going to be a long ride.

One great thing that did happen was that earlier that year I had talked with a teacher at Ashland Middle School about the Washington DC trip that had been canceled during James' eighth grade year because of the pandemic. I asked if they planned to go with this year's eighth grade class and if the kids who missed the trip could go with them. At the time, it seemed doubtful, but that changed—and James was able to go the summer after freshman year on a weeklong school history trip to Washington DC, Philadelphia, and New York City.

At the trip orientation, we found out they would be going to a Broadway play. I thought it would be amazing if it could be Hamilton. James had already watched the movie version of the original play about 40+ times and had memorized the entire script and every song—his ability to hyper focus when motivated is incredible. Later, when we got the finalized itinerary, we found out that the play they were going to see was indeed Hamilton. I teased him that he probably would get frowns from audience members if he sang along during the show. What an awesome blessing for him. He had a fantastic time and was so glad he got to experience it.

I had some inheritance from my uncle's estate, which sold in May. Although it was still in probate and would take several months to settle, so I could not spend the money yet. I proposed an offer to Mike for buying the house, but he didn't accept it. By the following January when the probate closed, we had still not come to an agreement, so I started looking for a place to live. Then we could sell the house. He had offered to let us stay if we paid mortgage, insurance, and taxes. Then we could sell when the kids finished school. I did not want to share ownership. The house still needed to be renovated to make more room for us, and I didn't want to invest money into a house that I would later have to split when it was sold. I wanted no ties outside of our children.

After winter break I was still not able to come to an agreement and the house search got serious. It was in mid-January when we decided to go look at a house up on the hill. It was a great house that I found listed in Ashland rentals online. I had called three times and didn't get a return call and James said let's drive by it. We had just looked at a place that the kids did not approve of, and I decided it wouldn't hurt to go look at the house on the hill from the outside. As we drove up, the owner, accompanied by his daughter, was unlocking the front door. I rolled down the window to let them know we were interested in the house but had not gotten a call back from the rental agency. He was a bit concerned about that, so he invited us in. It was an instant love at first sight for the kiddos.

The view was gorgeous and looked out on to the Cascade Range, specifically Grizzly Peak. The whole northern wall was bordering a wraparound porch with large windows and sliding glass doors, so there was a multitude of great views from all the rooms. The flooring was an elegant, brand new light oak with unique grain patterns and texture variations. There was a beautiful light tan stone fireplace, a captivating center-piece in the mid-century home that embodied the architec-tural charm and style of the era. It was a rustic, yet refined aesthetic that perfectly complemented the home's design.

There was a pool table in the family room next to a bedroom with its own bathroom. James claimed this room. The master bedroom also had an attached bathroom. I called dibs on that room. There was another bathroom across the hall from a third bedroom that was perfect for the girls. A garage for storage and a carport were both attached, with two acres of yard to explore.

The owner took a liking to us, so we filled out an applica-tion and he checked our references. Within two weeks we moved in on my birthday. Several members from our church came to help as a birthday present. It was an answer to our prayers. This would be a great place for entertaining friends and healing after a bitter divorce.

James immediately started inviting all his friends over and it seemed like there were teenagers coming and going all the time. I was happy to have them at our house though. They were all good kids and needed to have a safe place to hang out. There were many nights when his friends would gather around the dinner table with us and the conversation would get quite lively. We would joke that we should start a YouTube channel and call it "Dinner at the Robertson's." The laughter and topics were always plentiful and entertaining.

One night though, one of James' friends stopped by after I had gone to bed and took James out for a joyride. While driving behind Lithia Park on a gravel road, his friend slid and hit the dirt wall. His friend was only sixteen and had not had his license for very long, and would have gotten in trouble for driving a minor. At about midnight, I was awoken by James, and he said he needed to talk to me. He said he had done something bad and that I needed to come out to the living room. I got up and went out to hear what had happened. During his admission he had his hand covering his face. He slowly removed his hand to show a large gash near his eye and forehead. He tried to tell me that it wasn't that bad, but I disagreed. I quickly got dressed and took him to the emergency room at Ashland Asante Hospital. After five stitches, we returned home.

The boy's father called me the next day, hoping to settle this outside of insurance. I felt compassion for them and decided I would do this. The emergency room was paid, and James was not allowed to hang out with that kid anymore. I had hoped he had learned his lesson.

On the twins' eleventh birthday they hosted their first slumber party. It was fun having twelve preteens over. They played pool, jumped on the trampoline, painted nails, played on the VR, made jewelry, ate pizza, cake, and ice cream, danced, sang karaoke, and watched movies… They had so much fun.

The next morning, James was riding his bike to work, Rogue Credit Union. He had been working there for about three months. On the way down the hill, he crashed and hurt his leg. I am at home with the ten girls who had stayed the night and James came in the house claiming he had broken his leg. I told him it probably was not broken since he was able to walk up the hill with his bike. He put on the drama full force and said he needed to go to the ER.

I was between a rock and a hard place. I couldn't leave these ten girls alone, yet I saw the pain James was in. I called one of the parents and she said she would be right over to watch the girls. At that point I told the girls that they were not allowed to cook while I was gone. So I stopped the breakfast and drove James to emergency once again, only a month later than the last visit.

When I left, I was expecting the other mom would be there within a couple minutes, but it was more like twenty. In the meantime, a couple of the girls went into the kitchen and tried to finish the muffins I had started. They were put into the oven as the mom arrived. The kids then tried to make eggs, which turned out hard and rubbery and the muffins ended up getting burnt. The mom assumed I had directed the kids to finish breakfast because the girls had convinced her I had.

After James had an X-ray showing no broken bones, we returned to the house to find the kitchen a mess. Oh my, the fun of being a single mom. Besides the morning ordeal, the party was a success.

The following Lunar New Year we had another great party. This was an adult and kid party. Everyone brought an Asian dish (most homemade) and we passed out fortune cookies and red envelopes. The food was great and there was plenty of variety. The kids got ahold of some fireworks and poppers and had fun outside. Good times.

Chapter 24

I t's funny how life can seem as though everything is flowing, and then all of a sudden—it feels like the rug gets pulled out from under you.

About three weeks after we had moved into our new home, I was told that I might not have a job after the school year ended due to budget cuts. Pandemic funding had ended, and the district had to start saving money. I was one of the highest paid due to my experience and was nervous I would be let go since I was still in the probationary period of my employment.

Sure enough, when the administrators were told to make staff cuts, I became an easy target. The news was devastating. My kids and I had just settled into our new home, and the thought of uprooting them again broke my heart. They didn't want to leave, and neither did I. All I could think about was the tiny pool of available jobs in Southern Oregon, and the fear that I might not be able to provide for my family kept me up at night.

I have had so many great relationships with students and parents. I knew my work reflected by dedication and care to the students over the years. Over the next few months I was praised often for my work and teaching relationships by parents, teachers, students, and even the principal. Here are some letters I received:

Ms. Robertson,

I wanted to say thank you very much for everything you have done for Leo this year. He has grown, learned, felt heard/seen, and has truly blossomed with you as his teacher. Taking the time to come to his primary program meant a lot to him. He never came home and said he had had a bad day this whole school year which is amazing to me. I know he knew you cared about him personally and I think that really is what made him be able to relax and focus on learning. My kids said you aren't coming back to Jacksonville, and we are all quite sad about it. Gina was really hoping to have you for third grade. I hope wherever you go next is wonderful but always know you hold a special place in the Brown's heart. Again, thank you so much!

Ms. Robertson,

Thank you so much for such a wonderful year. I appreciate the love you gave Robbie. You were an answer to many prayers. We are so grateful he had you as a teacher. You are a light and a strength. Robbie admires you and I can't think of a better example for him to have. Thanks again for all you've done!

Ms. Robertson,

Thank you for an amazing year! Emily has loved being in your class and she just thinks the world of you, as do we. Have a wonderful summer!

I will miss you so much, Emily

Roses are red

Violets are blue

I wrote this poem just for you- Emily

Best teacher ever, Elsie

Not to mention a wall full of notes and cards from my students. I was truly loved and had a deep connection with this class. I still get emails from a student who was loving and highly intelligent.

My next plan was to apply for teaching positions in Ashland. I applied for eight different teaching jobs and got no response from the district or schools. Then a job opening came up at the beginning of the school year that I really wanted. It was an administrative position for the district as the Equity and Inclusion Administrator. This would be a dream job. I applied and had a great letter of recommendation from the BASE director. I heard nothing again. Then later I found out that the position was canceled, and the school district was not going to continue with an EDI liaison at all. It was being cut. Budget cuts were being made. It appeared that my experience was a handicap for finding a job post-pandemic. A time with limited monies.

My dad's house sold and I had money in the bank, so I decided to focus my attention on my kids and became a stay-at-home mom again. The following two school years would show this was a good move for our family. At least that was my feeling. Their father and I had different perspectives on such things, but we kept our children as the priority and focus. Problems come and go no matter what in this life. Staying neutral and observing is the calmest way to navigate through them. Unfortunately, this can be a challenge for some at times.

As the next school year progressed, I had grown aware of my fifteen-year-old son starting to date. This is such a bittersweet time for me as a mom. It tugs at my heart to see him taking those first steps into the complicated world of relationships, making choices about girls without my guidance. Part of me wants to hold on, to protect him from heartache or mistakes.

But another part knows I have to step back and let him find his own way. It's not easy to loosen my grip, but I know these experiences are a vital part of growing up. I want to respect his choices and support him, trusting that he's finding his own way. My hope is to stay connected with James as he navigates this chapter in his life. Even though letting go is difficult, I'm proud of the young man he's becoming—and I'll always be here to support him, quietly cheering him on from the sidelines.

Chapter 25

Divorce is not always easy. Although my kids seemed resilient, I had to learn how to control my emotions and try to keep uncomfortable communications from the kids. I wanted them to continue to have a relationship with their father. I did not want to interfere with that; however, it was difficult for me when I began receiving a high volume of unfiltered text messages from him. The constant messages became overwhelming and made it hard for me to focus on my work, adding another layer of stress to an already challenging time. At first, I would complain about them to my kids and then be told they didn't want to be in the middle of it. Such wise souls. They didn't need to be involved in our squabbles, and I realized this was something I needed to keep from them. I had to see it for what it was—navigating our new life. It was difficult to learn how not to discuss the unfiltered remarks with my children, but I needed to learn to contain it, and my sister became my outlet for this. I am still a work in progress, although, 98% of the time I am able to see his pain for what it really is and move on.

Their dad moved to a town about 30 minutes from Ashland. He now picks the girls up on Tuesday afternoons for dinner and some time together, in addition to every other Friday overnight. On Sundays, he takes James out for ultimate frisbee and dinner. We swap Thanksgiving and share Christmas break as well—usually spending Christmas day all together. While this arrangement isn't always ideal, it does give the kids the opportunity to stay connected with their father, which I know is extremely important for them. Having grown up in a divorced household myself, I truly understand the value of maintaining that relationship.

Raising a teenager and twins as a single mom has shown me many challenges to work through and overcome. Being an imperfect teen myself helped me to have more clarity on this time of motherhood. A big part of me didn't want to see my son make the same mistakes I did. Sometimes this played out as creating the opposite of what I had intended. The more I leaned into allowing him to experience life, the less he seemed to resist. Of course I had to guide as a parent; however, this guidance needed to give him room to grow and become his own authentic self. With guidance comes understanding and acceptance for your child's own sovereignty. A parent's job is not to mold, but to help them become adults and to shine their own light. I think this lesson can be very difficult to accept.

My girls, on the other hand, had the comfort of one another. As built-in friends, they always seemed able to keep each other amused, sharing inside jokes and laughter, often happy and carefree. Watching them together warmed my heart and brought smiles to my face, but I could also see subtle changes as they began to leave childhood behind. They were slowly turning into young women, and I knew the teenage years, especially thirteen, would probably bring challenges—both for them and me. I sometimes worried about how we would navigate that time, and I found myself hoping that all I was learning as a parent with James would somehow help me become a better, more understanding mom for my daughters as they moved through those tricky, transformative years.

As an adult, my experience has taught me wisdom I want to impart on my kids. Yet I've learned vicariously through my own children that true wisdom is not static or arrogant but rather is a continuous process of learning and humility that can change when open to new perspectives and observance. The more neutral we see the world, the more we are able to discern what is truth. I can't force my beliefs onto my children and have learned this through empathy and compassion for others. Sometimes I just need to let go and listen. I liken this to God giving His children free choice to learn from mistakes and still be there to show unconditional love.

One thing for sure is that each child came to Earth with their own personalities and gifts. These things can be built upon through experience. My daughters may be twins, but they are very much their own person. Eliza's love language is touch; she loves to give and receive hugs, and she has an incredible intuition for how others are feeling. She's often drawn to anyone in need of comfort or support. Zoey, on the other hand, thrives on words of affirmation. She is happiest when people offer her kindness and positive remarks. Although Zoey tends to be a bit more reserved than Eliza, she truly lights up when someone acknowledges her with warmth and encouragement, quickly becoming a loyal friend in return.

Both girls are very active, but Zoey seems to be especially athletic. She's always pushing herself to do her best, whether she's trying out a new sport or practicing her favorite activity.

Eliza enjoys being active as well—she's a master at the pogo stick and can bounce for what seems like forever! But when it comes to athletic drive and determination, Zoey truly shows her strength.

While their unique personalities and interests shine through, there's still a lot the girls share. Growing up, Eliza and Zoey have always been invited to all the same events and seem to get along with the same people, sharing one big friend group. But as they get older, I can see them starting to carve out their own individual paths. Zoey is becoming more interested in fashion and puts extra thought into what she wears, while Eliza is much more focused on just having fun and being herself, no matter what anyone thinks. It will be exciting to watch how their styles (and their personalities) keep evolving as they head into their teen years!

James always seemed to be an "old soul" and so I listened and learned from him throughout his childhood. Once he became a teen, I had to remind myself of this. Teen parenting is quite different than parenting younger children. They are becoming adults at a much more rapid pace. However, their brains are not fully developed. That being said, James knows himself better than anyone else. Sometimes his choices are not always ideal, but he understands who he is, thus the "old soul" paradigm.

As I watch my beautiful children grow and explore their interests, it feels like living inside a wonderful adventure story. Each new experience and every challenge they face helps shape who they are becoming, and somehow, it always manages to bring us even closer together. Our lives here in

Ashland have blended into a colorful patchwork of activities, discoveries, and hilarious moments, from epic competitions of all sorts to spontaneous dance parties and heartfelt sibling teamwork. All these shared adventures have strengthened our family bond, making our days brighter and our memories even sweeter. And while the joyful moments are easy to cherish, I've also come to see how our trials—however small or daunting—have taught us invaluable lessons and pulled us together in unexpected ways.

One of the most significant challenges we've faced recently has been supporting James through his ADHD diagnosis. James thinks differently than many children his age. There is a part of him that is carefree and childlike, and at the same time wise beyond his years. He is a child full of rapid brain movement. This can be very beneficial when downloading information. It can also get him into trouble because he is quick to take dares. He self-diagnosed himself as ADHD when he was fourteen. I did not see this and had difficulty accepting it, but I made the appointment for him to be evaluated. He was found to have ADHD by his teachers and doctors—diagnosed with combined ADHD, since he is easily distracted and impulsive. He tried medication for about 3-4 days and decided he didn't like how it made him drowsy and his stomach upset. He did say it helped him concentrate a bit more.

He would often do things impulsively to get laughs. In school this would sometimes get him in trouble. His friends would dare him to do silly things, and if it didn't go against his own better judgment, he would do it. Social media pranks exacerbated this. The latest trends were fodder for him. The ALS ice bucket challenge from when he was eight to creating cool video trends that appear as magic after editing. For a couple years he was certain he would be a video gamer and go on to college to major in this, and even proved to me that this was a growing major among colleges.

During his freshman year when he was suspended for carrying a pocketknife, he reasoned that he only carried it so that when he went downtown after school, he would have protection from people he perceived as hostile—whether because of racist views or encounters with individuals struggling with their mental health. I reasoned that he knew karate and could run fast. These days, with school shootings becoming more common, carrying anything that can be considered a weapon is not acceptable in school. He rebutted this claiming it was another good reason to carry a knife for protection at school. I think back to when I was in high school; pick-up trucks with gun racks displaying guns were commonplace in the school parking lot. I guess it's all perspective.

His sophomore year, he was talked into driving a carload of friends through town for a "joyride"; it was an out period and against his better judgment, he conceded. They were driving on a winding gravel road when the back-heavy car skidded backwards, rolling down an embankment above Lithia Park and totaling his Mini Cooper. Several of his friends were injured, one needing to be flown to Portland for emergency surgery. And it was not legal for him to drive anyone but adults and siblings for the first six months of his license. It had been less than a month. Albeit this was not a law when I was a new driver, it was the law now, nonetheless. Can you say, "Squirrel!?"

This experience proved to be a very dark time in our lives. James' impulsive efforts to try to make things right were misunderstood, even though he genuinely cared about what had happened. Unfortunately, this misunderstanding created distance between our families and weighed heavily on James, leading him into a period of deep sadness. It took me time to work through the anger, sadness, and even guilt I felt for buying him the car—I couldn't help but wonder if he had even learned from the previous car accident.

It was after these events that I realized that I might want to educate myself on ADHD. I read three books and took two classes that summer. I had a better understanding of my son as well as the negativity associated with ADHD. I came to realize this was a misnomer. His neurodiversity actually was a gift that gave him an ability to multitask, learn quickly when interested, and be a natural for entrepreneurship. It was an aha moment for me. He wasn't a label, he was unique in his way of seeing the world. I had often dismissed his ability to multitask because in my world, people couldn't really do that successfully. He hated reading but was able to speed read. He could see absurdities in the world that others couldn't or wouldn't.

He also has the ability to hyperfocus. If he is interested in something, he can accomplish a significant amount of work in a short period of time. He can emerge himself in his learning to the point of deep understanding and mastery. The intense concentration associated with hyperfocus can lead to innovation and creativity. This is his superpower. He already has created something for the martial arts world for which he is currently waiting for a patent.

When Zoey was five, she became interested in martial arts from watching *Kung Fu Panda*. She would pray to God often to let her learn karate. After a while I couldn't stand this cuteness any longer, so I looked into karate classes in Ashland. I came across a place owned by the karate legend, Hanshi Jerry Piddington. It seemed like a good place to get started, so I signed her up for a three-month introductory class.

She was so happy and began to improve in her listening and self-discipline. One day James said he wanted to learn as well. After discussing cost with Hanshi, we were talked into the family deal. Now Zoey, James, Eliza, and I were all registered in karate. This became an almost daily commitment. The girls were in a class for 4 to 7-year-olds called Little Dragons and James and I were in the beginner's class. As a family we now spent many hours at karate class each week. We were now known as the karate family. Lessons, practice, tests, competitions, and camps. We were in deep. Some are soccer moms; I was a karate mom.

Over a period of seven years, our family fluctuated in and out of karate. When the pandemic hit two years in, we took some time off but started up again full time once masks were no longer mandatory. Once Eliza got to green belt, she decided it wasn't fun anymore and decided to quit. A few months later I quit because the new ownership was not fun for me either. I was working hard, but perfection was not something that I could achieve and I was no longer enjoying the training.

James was starting to feel the same, only he was about to test for his black belt, so he stuck it out. He continued for a couple more months after the test but gradually stopped feeling the joy and connection to the sensei. He decided to move on from her class, though he still loved karate. I wished there was another martial arts place nearby that he would join, but he is not interested in the few places near us.

Now it was only Zoey left, and she continued for another ten months on her own. However, she could not make the camp test for her brown stripe due to a scheduling conflict with a girls' camp she had been planning to attend through our church that was already paid for. I asked the sensei for a private test, and she said that she would not do private tests for brown and black belts. I thought this was odd since James had had a private test when he received his brown stripe when he had a scheduling conflict. And she had no problem that year giving James a private test.

I let Zoey know what her sensei said and also that if she did not attend the camp trip to test she would have to wait another year for the next camp. This would mean she would now be a year behind her three friends who would go on to test for black belt the following year. This news was very upsetting to Zoey. She had worked hard the past year and knew all her material well.

I suggested that she talk to her sensei to see if she could change her mind. The day this conversation occurred,

Zoey came out of karate very upset and feeling like she was going to throw up. I suggested that maybe she could split the camps. The girls' camp was Wednesday through Saturday, and the karate camp was Friday night through Sunday. I thought maybe she could leave the girls' camp early Saturday, and I could drive her to the karate camp for Saturday and Sunday testing. She was not sure she even wanted to stay in karate at this point. I told her the choice was up to her and to think about it before making a decision.

It ended up that the other sensei rallied around Zoey and convinced the dojo owner to let her have a private test. I was so excited for her, but she was so upset that all this had happened that she said she wanted to quit. Her brother tried to talk her into at least sticking with it through the test and then maybe take some time off. She would not budge. She said, "I know enough karate to protect myself and I don't care about getting my black belt."

So that was that. She had made her decision and would not be talked out of it by anyone. Even her best friend begged her to stay. She is so good at karate, but I understood and supported her. She was quite pleased with her decision and felt justified.

My kids are quite musical. Besides loving to sing, they have all dabbled in various instruments. James started ukulele lessons in third grade. Once he had mastered a few songs he would go to Lithia Park and do some busking. It was super fun to see the excitement in his eyes when someone would put money in his ukulele case. In sixth grade he started violin lessons at the school. By seventh grade his ukulele lessons morphed into guitar lessons online with the same teacher during the pandemic. Eventually he started lessons at Guitar Center in eighth grade. Zoey was interested in guitar as well and started electric guitar lessons. Eliza followed suit and began piano lessons there also.

At home we had an organ that the kids would gather around, and James would play guitar, while Eliza would play the organ and Zoey would sing. Later Eliza got a keyboard to replace the organ for her at home practice.

Eventually I decided to take guitar lessons at Guitar Center with them. At first I played acoustic, but then one day my teacher talked me into trying electric. I fell in love with the strings being closer together and switched. We joked about starting a band and calling ourselves The Neapolitans—because we are three different colors. It was not to be though.

After freshman year James decided he didn't want to continue violin, although the twins joined fifth grade orchestra and began playing the viola. Halfway through his sophomore year he lost interest in guitar lessons as well. He did continue to play on occasion. Not sure if he will continue in the future. He seemed to pick up the guitar easily and I wished he had stuck with it.

The twins will be teenagers this year and I am sure that will be a book in itself.

They started puberty when they were ten and are now both taller than me. They are starting to show signs of teen spirit, and I pray that it's more entertaining than drama. We'll see.

Chapter 26

As I look back on my road to parenthood, I realize that all the loss and pain were, in a way, necessary steps along my journey. It was only through these experiences that I was able to let go of the dream of having biological children and open myself to the idea of international adoption. Though I wouldn't wish infertility on anyone, I realize now that it is a very real part of the human experience. Becoming a mother has brought me so much joy and laughter—sprinkled with some difficulties—but I know without a doubt, it has all been so worth the journey.

I know that my path was carved out to help others who may be experiencing similar trials and tribulations on their own unique journey. We are all here to serve one another in different ways, and I believe this is what truly bonds us as human beings.

James is my first, and this will always be our special bond. He is an old soul with so much to offer the world. He is brave and courageous. He has experienced so much for a young man, yet he has persevered through it all. His many talents and bright mind continue to amaze me. I can't wait to see him grow into the man he is meant to be. I'm sure whatever he endeavors, he will power through and come out on top. My son and my dream come true—I love him forever.

Eliza is a light and a joy in this world. Her countenance is brighter than a field of sunflowers in full bloom—my favorite flower. Her smile is contagious, spreading joy to everyone around her. Her warmth and good cheer radiate throughout the room, touching all those in her presence. Her beauty abounds and her talents are undeniable, yet it's her emotional intelligence that sets her apart from all the others. She is a rare gem—radiant, unforgettable, and truly one of a kind—my forever love.

And then there is Zoey. Zoey has taught me so much over the years—from her curiosity to take everything apart, to learning her love language and how best to speak with her. She is quiet yet loud, smart yet hardworking, beautiful though she doesn't always see it herself. Sometimes, I see myself in her; in fact, others have said the same. Even though we aren't blood related, we're starting to look alike—in our manner-isms, at least. She is my mini-me and my mom is laughing up in heaven—forever in love.

I have so much gratitude for my journey on the road to parenthood. I wouldn't change motherhood for becoming a DINK again, or anything else for that matter. I am changed forever yet coming back to myself at the same time. If you are considering parenthood or have had difficulties with it, I hope that this book has helped you. At times I was frustrated and wondered why I was writing this book—my counselor and friends said it is an inspirational story, and I need to write about it. That was my goal, to inspire, and I hope it worked.

Best wishes for your journey. Love and peace, sprinkled with joy.

About the Author

Barbara Robertson is a passionate educator, devoted mother of three, and an inspiring voice in the world of parenting. With over 20 years of experience teaching kindergarten through eighth grade, Barbara has touched countless lives both in and out of the classroom. Her journey as a mother and educator has fueled her desire to support others along their own road to parenthood. An aspiring author and podcast host, Barbara weaves together her deep faith and experience to encourage, uplift, and inspire families. She lives in beautiful Ashland, Oregon, where she continues to share her wisdom and warmth with her community—and now, with readers everywhere.

www.ingramcontent.com/pod-product-compliance
Lightning Source LLC
Chambersburg PA
CBHW070908130626
46555CB00001B/52